HOME REPAIR AND IMPROVEMENT

SHELVES AND CABINETS

TIME®
LIFE
BOOKS

Other Publications
VOICES OF THE CIVIL WAR
THE TIME-LIFE COMPLETE GARDENER
JOURNEY THROUGH THE MIND AND BODY
WEIGHT WATCHERS® SMART CHOICE RECIPE COLLECTION
TRUE CRIME
THE AMERICAN INDIANS
THE ART OF WOODWORKING
LOST CIVILIZATIONS
ECHOES OF GLORY
THE NEW FACE OF WAR
HOW THINGS WORK
WINGS OF WAR
CREATIVE EVERYDAY COOKING
COLLECTOR'S LIBRARY OF THE UNKNOWN
CLASSICS OF WORLD WAR II
TIME-LIFE LIBRARY OF CURIOUS AND UNUSUAL FACTS
AMERICAN COUNTRY
VOYAGE THROUGH THE UNIVERSE
THE THIRD REICH
MYSTERIES OF THE UNKNOWN
TIME FRAME
FIX IT YOURSELF
FITNESS, HEALTH AND NUTRITION
SUCCESSFUL PARENTING
HEALTHY HOME COOKING
UNDERSTANDING COMPUTERS
LIBRARY OF NATIONS
THE ENCHANTED WORLD
THE KODAK LIBRARY OF CREATIVE PHOTOGRAPHY
GREAT MEALS IN MINUTES
THE CIVIL WAR
PLANET EARTH
COLLECTOR'S LIBRARY OF THE CIVIL WAR
THE EPIC OF FLIGHT
THE GOOD COOK
WORLD WAR II
THE OLD WEST

*For information on and a full description
of any of the Time-Life Books series listed above,
please call 1-800-621-7026 or write:*
Reader Information
Time-Life Customer Service
P.O. Box C-32068
Richmond, Virginia 23261-2068

SHELVES AND CABINETS

BY THE EDITORS OF TIME-LIFE BOOKS, ALEXANDRIA, VIRGINIA

The Consultants

Jeff Palumbo is a registered journeyman carpenter who has a home-building and remodeling business in northern Virginia. His interest in carpentry was sparked by his grandfather, a master carpenter with more than 50 years' experience. Mr. Palumbo teaches in the Fairfax County Adult Education Program.

Len Singer was trained as a cabinetmaker. He owns LMS Woodworking, Inc., a general contractor specializing in the design and construction of additions and restorations to historic homes in the greater Washington, D.C., area.

Mark M. Steele is a professional home inspector in the Washington, D.C., area. He has developed and conducted training programs in home-ownership skills for first-time homeowners. He appears frequently on television and radio as an expert in home repair and other consumer topics.

CONTENTS

1 TECHNIQUES AND REMEDIES — 6

Hand Tools for Cabinetry — 8

Power Tools for the Home Workshop — 10

Techniques for Cutting Joints — 16

Refurbishing Cabinets — 20

2 SHELVES FOR EVERY PURPOSE — 34

Planning a Project — 36

Simple, All-Purpose Shelving — 38

A Shelf on Sturdy Brackets — 43

Floating Shelves — 46

Shelving for a Wall — 50

3 CABINETS AND WALL SYSTEMS — 56

Planning a Cabinet — 58

Building the Cabinet Carcass — 62

Framing the Cabinet Front — 66

Making and Installing Drawers — 72

Making and Hanging Cabinet Doors — 78

A Versatile Wall System — 90

A Compact Computer Center — 92

A Bookcase Accompaniment — 97

An Adaptation for a Television — 99

4 FINISHING TOUCHES — 102

Dressing Up the Finished Piece — 104

Smoothing the Surface — 108

Filling Wood for Sheen and Color — 110

Staining Richness into Wood — 112

Penetrating Oils — 114

A Hard-Wearing Finish — 116

5 APPENDIX — 118

Wall Fasteners — 119

Types of Wood — 120

Wood Grading — 122

Choosing the Right Finish — 124

Index — 126

Acknowledgments — 128

Picture Credits — 128

1

Techniques and Remedies

Precision not only is the key to making a well-built cabinet with doors and drawers that open and close freely, but also pays off with even the simplest repairs. This chapter first shows you the tools you'll need to do expert cabinetry and the fundamentals of their use, then explains how to bring off a variety of remedies that can give new life to a favorite piece of furniture.

Hand Tools for Cabinetry   8

Power Tools for the Home Workshop   10

Circular Saws
Table Saws
Using the Rip Fence
Saber Saws
Variable-Speed Drills
High-Speed Routers

Techniques for Cutting Joints   16

Rabbets and Dadoes with a Router
Preparing a Table Saw for Joinery
Making the Cuts

Refurbishing Cabinets   20

Unsticking Drawers
Building Up a Worn Drawer Runner
Replacing a Runner
Repairing Drawer Guides and Bottoms
Rebuilding a Drawer
Diagnosing and Solving Door Problems
Shimming a Hinge
Deepening a Hinge Mortise
Accommodating a Warped Door
Freeing a Sticky Door
A Quick Fix for Shelves
Substituting Shelves for Drawers
Switching to Drawers from Shelves

Taking apart a dovetailed drawer →

Hand Tools for Cabinetry

Along with the basic hand tools found in most home workshops, the specialized tools shown here are needed for many of the projects in this book. All but the French and flexible curves are available at hardware stores; the curves are sold in art-supply shops.

Always use these tools in accordance with the manufacturer's specifications, and keep them in good repair: Periodically sharpen saw blades and plane blades to ensure that they cut evenly (your hardware dealer or the manufacturer can supply sharpening instructions). From time to time, check the try and combination squares to make sure that hard handling has not affected their alignment.

JACK PLANE

BLOCK PLANE

RABBET PLANE

Planes.

A jack plane, held with both hands, is used to shave wood from long or broad surfaces. A palm-sized block plane serves for tighter spots. To shave lipped doors or other notched surfaces, use a rabbet plane; its blade is exposed, allowing you to remove wood right up to the edge of a rabbet.

COMBINATION SQUARE

FRENCH CURVE

Marking tools.

Both a try square and a combination square are used to mark lines perpendicular to the edge of a piece of wood. A combination square can also rule 45-degree lines. For drawing free-form shapes, use a French curve, made of rigid plastic, or a flexible curve, which consists of bendable wires sheathed in plastic.

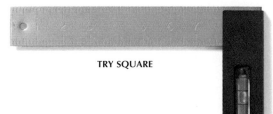

TRY SQUARE

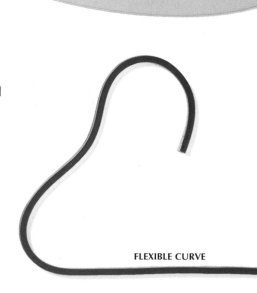

FLEXIBLE CURVE

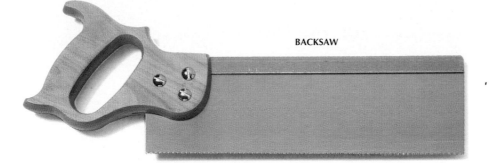

BACKSAW

Saws.

A backsaw, possessing a reinforced spine to keep its cuts straight, is used in conjunction with a miter box. A keyhole saw, with its tapered end, is made for work in cramped spaces. A coping saw has a very thin, flexible blade that can make sharply curved cuts, such as those needed when shaping interior miters in molding.

KEYHOLE SAW

COPING SAW

HAND-SCREW CLAMP

C CLAMP

Clamps.

A C clamp holds together relatively narrow pieces of wood at a single point on each side. For clamping larger assemblies such as drawers, use a pipe clamp; the fittings and pipe are sold separately, allowing you to construct a clamp of any length. A hand-screw clamp, with its flat jaws, applies pressure over a wide area; because the jaws work independently, you can clamp unevenly shaped pieces.

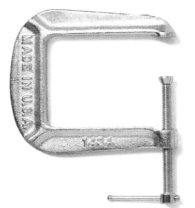

PIPE CLAMP

From table saws to routers to drills, power tools are indispensable aids for any project. The machines shown on these and the following pages save time and can help even novices toward accurate results.

The Right Tools: At hardware and home-supply stores, you should be able to find high-quality tools at moderate prices. Purchase tools of capacity and power sufficient for the work you plan to do. Double-insulated plastic casings help to prevent electrical shock, and permanently lubricated bearings simplify tool care.

Just as important as buying a good tool is using the right tool for the job. A saber saw, for example, is designed for cutting curves *(page 14)*. Although it can also make a long, straight cut through plywood, the result from a circular saw or a table saw will be cleaner and more precise *(pages 10-13)*. For maximum precision, use a table saw whenever possible.

All power tools come with instructions. Take the time to read them, then practice with the tools before beginning work.

POWER TOOL PRECAUTIONS

Safety is as important as skill in the operation of power tools, and there are a few rules that apply in every situation:

✔ Dress for the job. Avoid loose clothing, tuck in your shirt, and roll up your sleeves. Tie back long hair. Do not wear gloves—they reduce dexterity and can catch in moving parts.

✔ Wear eye protection. To keep wood dust and shavings out of your eyes, always wear goggles when using a power tool.

✔ Keep the work steady. Be sure to work on a stable surface. Clamp materials to the work surface whenever practical.

✔ Stand comfortably. Do not reach any farther than feels natural and never position yourself directly in front of or behind a moving saw.

✔ Recruit a helper. When making long cuts in boards or plywood, have a helper support the work. Sagging wood can jam a circular saw blade and tip over a table saw.

✔ Unplug idle tools. Disconnect power tools when you are finished with them; be certain to unplug tools whenever you make an adjustment or change bits or blades.

CIRCULAR SAWS

Anatomy of a circular saw.

The standard circular saw holds a $7\frac{1}{2}$-inch blade, which cuts wood up to 2 inches thick. A spring-activated guard rotates into the saw housing as a cut is begun and automatically covers the blade as the cut is finished. The angle-adjustment knob tilts the saw's base—called the shoe plate— up to 45 degrees, and another knob allows you to change the cutting depth *(opposite)*. An arbor bolt holds the blade in place and unscrews to change blades. To help prevent binding, buy a saw that develops at least $1\frac{1}{2}$ horsepower.

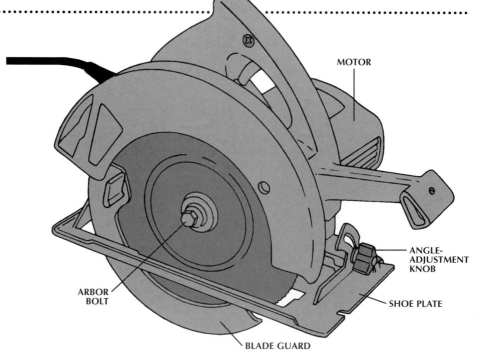

MOTOR

ANGLE-ADJUSTMENT KNOB

SHOE PLATE

ARBOR BOLT

BLADE GUARD

Blade styles.

A circular—or table—saw blade with the proper number of teeth reduces splintering as the blade exits the wood. A blade for plywood, whose thin outer plies splinter readily, has about 150 teeth. Cutting across the grain calls for a crosscut blade with at least 40 teeth; rip blades have only about 20 teeth. Combination blades, for both ripping and crosscutting, have sections of fine teeth separated by wide gaps called gullets.

Sawteeth flare out slightly in both directions to facilitate cutting *(inset)*. The coarser the teeth, the wider the flare, called the set, and the wider the cut, called the kerf.

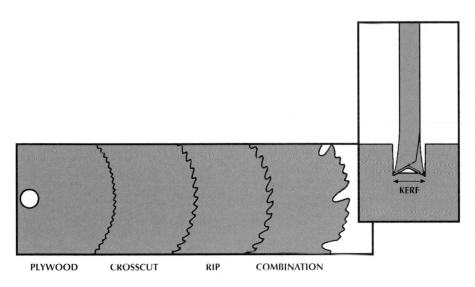

PLYWOOD   CROSSCUT   RIP   COMBINATION

KERF

Adjusting the blade depth.

◆ Raise the blade guard and place the saw on the board to be cut with the blade against the end. (Release the guard; the board will prevent it from closing.)
◆ Loosen the depth-adjustment knob.
◆ Then raise or lower the saw until the blade is about $\frac{1}{4}$ inch below the bottom of the board.
◆ Retighten the depth-adjustment knob.

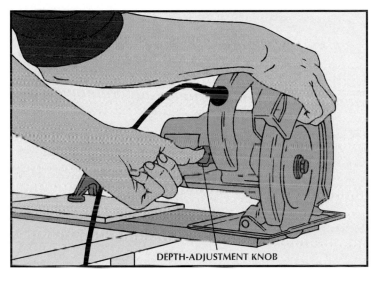

DEPTH-ADJUSTMENT KNOB

Sawing with a guide.

Since circular saws cut on the up-stroke, always cut wood with the good side down.
◆ Clamp a guide—the factory edge of a piece of plywood works well—on the workpiece so the kerf falls just on the waste side of the cutting line.
◆ Turn on the saw. Keeping the side of the shoe plate against the straightedge *(right),* cut slowly through the board. Do not force the blade—it may bind. For long cuts, have a helper support the waste portion and catch it when the cut is complete.

To cut a large plywood panel, rest it atop 2-by-4s set on the floor *(inset).*

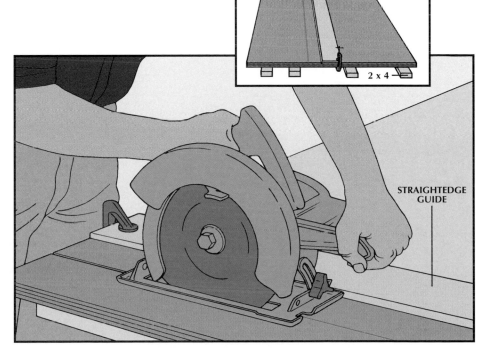

2 x 4

STRAIGHTEDGE GUIDE

TABLE SAWS

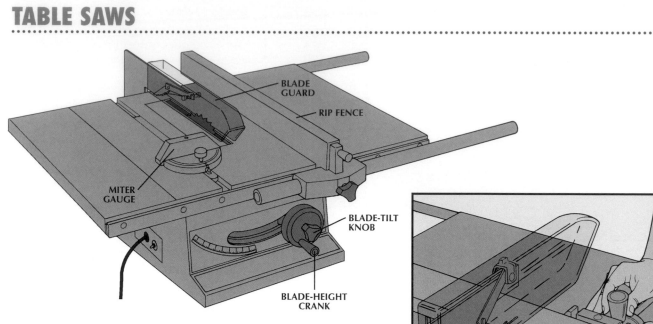

BLADE
GUARD

RIP FENCE

MITER
GAUGE

BLADE-TILT
KNOB

BLADE-HEIGHT
CRANK

A saw for precision cuts.

With its built-in guides, the table saw sets up quickly for both square and angled cuts. Furthermore, it cuts much more accurately than the hand-held circular saw. Available in full-size and tabletop models, a typical table saw uses 10-inch blades that cut $3\frac{1}{2}$ inches deep. Since table-saw blades cut on the downstroke, cut plywood with the good side up.

A metal rip fence, adjustable along guide bars, ensures a straight cut. There is also a pivoting miter gauge, which slides along a slot in the table, that feeds boards into the blade at any angle. Two controls, the blade-tilt knob and blade-height crank, adjust the angle and height of the blade itself. A table insert, which keeps sawdust from falling into the motor, is removable for changing blades. For safety, a plastic guard covers the blade.

Making a crosswise cut.

◆ Slide the rip fence out of the way.
◆ Adjust the blade height until the teeth are about $\frac{1}{4}$ inch higher than the workpiece.
◆ Set the edge of the board against the miter gauge, positioning it so that the blade falls on the waste side of the cutting line. Make sure the blade is not touching the board before proceeding.
◆ Switch on the saw. Holding the board against the miter gauge, use the gauge to push the board into the blade.
◆ When the cut is complete, turn off the saw and pull the board sideways to free it from the blade. Remove the waste piece from the table.

USING THE RIP FENCE

RIP FENCE-
LOCKING KNOB

1. Setting up the saw.

◆ Adjust the height of the blade so it extends about $\frac{1}{4}$ inch above the workpiece.
◆ Loosen the rip fence-locking knob.
◆ Adjust the fence so that its distance from the blade equals the distance between the edge of the workpiece and the cutting line. Make sure the blade falls just on the waste side of the line.
◆ Tighten the locking knob.

2. Making the cut.

◆ Turn on the saw.

◆ While holding the wood against the fence, push it forward into the blade. Near the end of the cut, advance the wood with a push stick *(inset)*, which is made by sawing a 90-degree notch in the end of a 1-by-2. Push the workpiece well past the blade before turning off the saw.

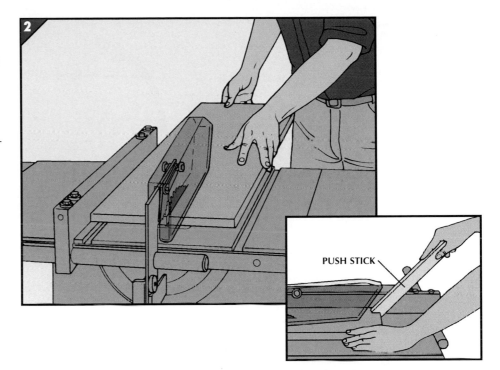

PUSH STICK

TRICKS OF THE TRADE

How to Get More Accurate Cuts

A device called a featherboard keeps wood from shifting and kicking back as it passes through a table saw. To construct one, first cut an end of a 16-inch-long piece of 1-by-3 hardwood at a 60-degree angle. Then make the "feathers" by cutting parallel slots into the mitered end at $\frac{1}{4}$-inch intervals.

To use the featherboard, first protect the rip fence by clamping or screwing an auxiliary wooden fence to it. Then clamp the featherboard to the auxiliary fence with its leading edge 2 inches from the blade and the feathers resting on the workpiece. As you push the wood into the saw blade, the springy feathers hold the board down. And since the feathers are bent and angled toward the blade, they prevent the wood from kicking back toward the operator.

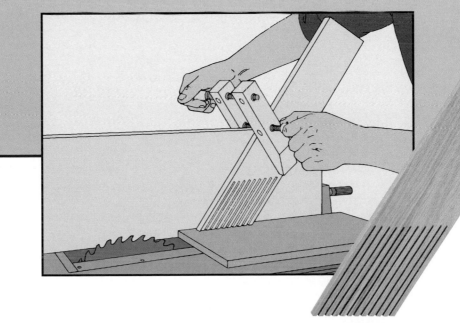

FEATHERBOARD

SABER SAWS

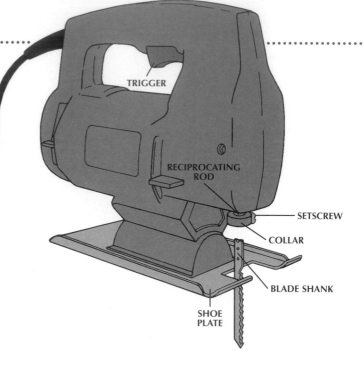

A saw for intricate cutting.

With its narrow, maneuverable blade, the saber saw is ideal for making curved cuts. A trigger in the handle turns the saw on and off and regulates the cutting speed—fast for straighter cuts, slower for more tightly curved ones. To insert a blade, first loosen the setscrew on the collar of the reciprocating rod. Then push the blade's notched shank as far as it will go into the reciprocating rod, and retighten the setscrew. Since the blade cuts on the upstroke, work with the good surface of the wood down to prevent tearing on that side.

Cutting a curved pattern.

Plan the cut to avoid moving the saw through impossibly tight turns. If the pattern has sharp corners, like the one at left, cut into each corner from opposite directions. And for patterns longer than a foot or two, make a few straight cuts, called relief cuts, through the waste section from the edge to the cutting line. As the saw hits each relief cut the waste falls away, preventing large waste sections from bending the wood and binding the blade.

◆ Rest the tip of the shoe plate on the wood, making sure the blade is not touching it.

◆ Start the saw, and guide the blade into the wood, swinging the back of the saw to the right or left as you move into curves. Do not force the blade; it may bind or break. If you end a cut with the blade in the wood, let the blade come to a stop before withdrawing it.

VARIABLE-SPEED DRILLS

Boring holes with ease.

Available in cordless and plug-in models, variable-speed drills turn faster the farther you pull the trigger. Most accept bits with a maximum shank diameter of $\frac{3}{8}$ inch, but through various tip designs these bits can bore holes up to about $1\frac{1}{2}$ inches across. To insert a bit, hand-turn the chuck collar to open the jaws, place the bit between the jaws, and tighten the chuck collar, again by hand. Then clamp the jaws tightly on the bit with the chuck key (right).

The twist bit shown at right is the standard bit for drilling through both wood and metal; the combination bit automatically drills counterbored pilot holes for screws. Bits are also available to drill holes in masonry and glass, as well as to drive screws.

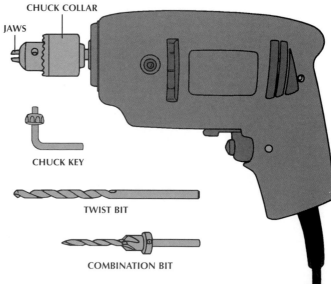

A Quick-Tightening Drill Chuck

If you use your power drill often and it has a keyed chuck, consider replacing it with a keyless one. Specially designed to grip a bit securely with hand-tightening alone, keyless chucks make fast work of changing bits. Although many new drill models are sold with a keyless chuck attached, older drills are easily converted by detaching the old chuck and screwing the new one onto the drill-motor shaft.

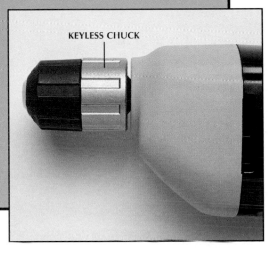

KEYLESS CHUCK

HIGH-SPEED ROUTERS

A tool for joinery and shaping.

Spinning razor-sharp bits at more than 25,000 rpm, a router makes quick work of carving out joints and shaping contours in wood. The tool consists of a motor mounted vertically on a two-handle base. Look for a router with a motor of at least $\frac{3}{4}$ horsepower. At the bottom of the motor shaft is a sleeve called a collet that secures the bit. A depth-adjustment knob raises and lowers the collet, and the clamp lever locks the bit at the chosen depth.

The most versatile joinery bit is the straight bit (in set, left), which cuts dadoes and rabbets. However, this bit needs a straightedge clamped to the workpiece to guide the router. More convenient for cutting rabbets is the rabbeting bit, with its built-in pilot that steers the router along the edge of the wood—eliminating the need for a guide.

The key to smooth router operation is to grip the tool firmly and move it steadily from left to right: Pushed too fast it loses speed and chews out big bites; pushed slowly, the bit scrapes the wood and tends to bounce off the cut.

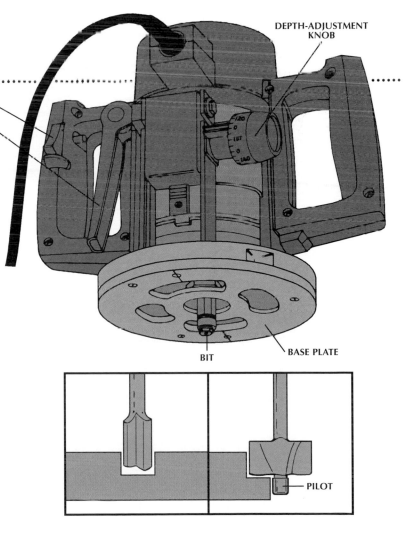

DEPTH-ADJUSTMENT KNOB

ON/OFF SWITCH

CLAMP LEVER

BIT

BASE PLATE

PILOT

The two most useful woodworking joints are stepped edges called rabbets, and grooves known as dadoes *(below, right)*. These classic joints strengthen a cabinet by increasing the gluing area. Furthermore, rabbets and dadoes make the pieces easier to assemble and align.

A Choice of Tools: You can cut rabbets and dadoes with a router or a table saw. The standard router technique for both rabbets and dadoes calls for using a straight bit *(page 15)* and a straightedge guide to keep the cut even *(opposite)*. For rabbets you can also use a rabbeting bit, which has a built-in guide *(page 15)*.

To cut these joints with a table saw, fit it with a dado head—an adjustable assembly of inner blades called chippers sandwiched between a pair of combination blades *(page 18)*, purchased as a kit. When cutting rabbets with a dado head, a notched auxiliary fence is required to protect the rip fence *(page 19)*.

Cutting Joints Efficiently: Whichever tool you use, draw all the cutting lines on every piece of wood before making any cuts. If you use a table saw, set the blade and rip fence for one type of cut, then cut all pieces with the same joint before resetting the blade and fence. On each piece, cut the rabbet joints first. Double-check the positions of the dadoes, then cut the dadoes that run across the wood grain. Finish by cutting the dadoes that run with the grain.

⚠️ **CAUTION** *When cutting rabbets and dadoes with a table saw, the blade guard must be removed. Work with caution around the exposed blade.*

SAFETY TIPS

Safety goggles protect your eyes when you are working with power tools. In an enclosed space, ear plugs reduce the noise of power tools to a safe level.

Rabbets and dadoes.

Rabbets *(below)* are most commonly cut into cabinet sides to conceal the edges of the back. Dadoes *(bottom)* are often cut in the sides of cabinets to anchor shelving, and in the top and bottom to hold vertical partitions. Although joint width depends on the thickness of the wood that fits into it, the standard depth for both joints is $\frac{3}{8}$ inch.

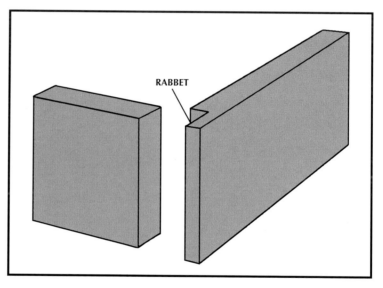

RABBET

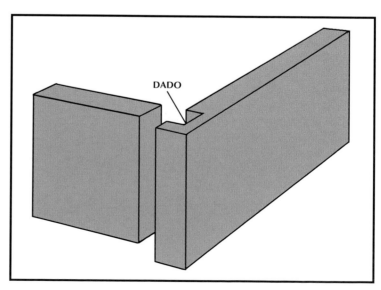

DADO

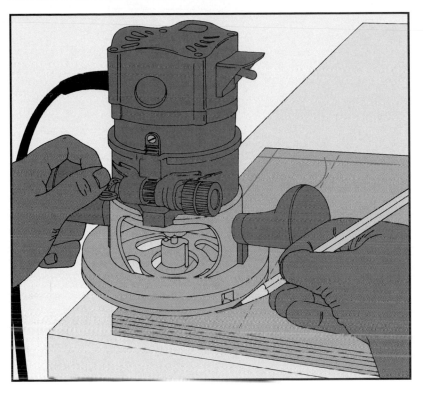

Positioning a guide.

◆ Mark the width of the rabbet or the dado on the board.

◆ Select a bit equal in diameter to the width of the joint. Mount the bit in the router, and set it flush with the base plate. Place the router on the board with the bit centered in the joint.

◆ Outline the router base on the board. Then move the router to the far end of the joint and draw a second outline. With a straightedge, draw a guideline that touches both outlines (dotted line, left).

◆ Select a straight board a few inches longer than the joint and wax the edge. Clamp the workpiece to the bench, then clamp or tack the board to the workpiece with its waxed edge along the guideline. To prevent splintering, secure a piece of scrap wood against the end of the workpiece.

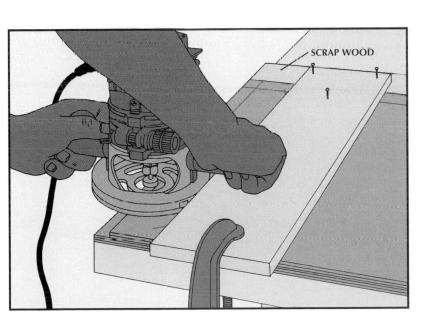

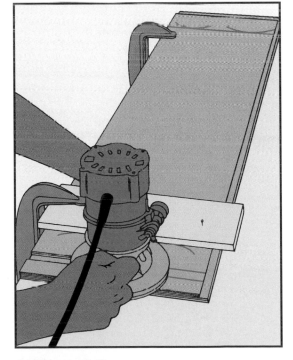

Cutting a rabbet.

◆ Set the router base against the guide, with the bit clear of the wood.

◆ Turn on the router and push the bit into the wood. Move the router slowly along the guide board to the end of the cut.

Cutting a dado.

◆ Place the router with its base against the guide and its bit clear of the left edge of the workpiece.

◆ Turn on the router and move the bit through the wood, holding the router base plate against the guide until the bit clears the right edge of the board.

Installing a dado head.

The outside blades and chippers of a dado head each cut a kerf $\frac{1}{16}$ inch wide, allowing you to cut dadoes of any multiple of that width. For intermediate widths, insert paper washers, provided with the dado head, between the chippers.

◆ Pull out the table insert and remove the standard blade from the arbor.

◆ Slip an outside blade over the arbor, followed by the necessary number of chippers and washers and the other ouside blade. Replace the arbor washer, and screw the arbor nut loosely in place.

◆ Rotate the blades so that the larger teeth of one outside blade are opposite the smaller teeth of the other, and the chippers line up with the gullets of both blades *(inset)*. Tighten the arbor nut.

◆ Replace the standard table insert with a dado insert having a wider slot.

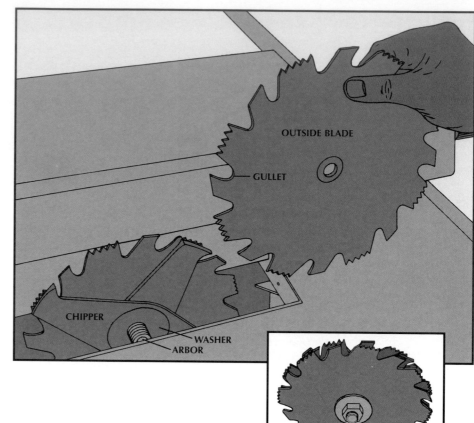

Notching a fence for rabbets.

◆ Install a $\frac{1}{4}$-inch-wide dado head on the saw and lower it to the level of the table.

◆ Fit the metal rip fence with a wood auxiliary fence cut from a 1-by-6. Position the new fence so it just overlaps the entire dado head.

◆ Turn on the saw and slowly raise the dado head about $\frac{1}{2}$ inch to cut a rounded notch in the wooden fence (left). Then turn off the saw and retract the blade.

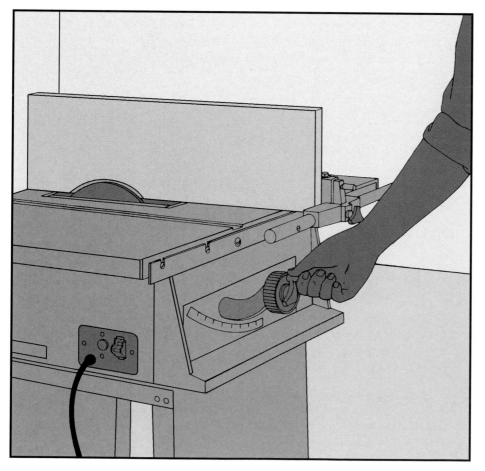

MAKING THE CUTS

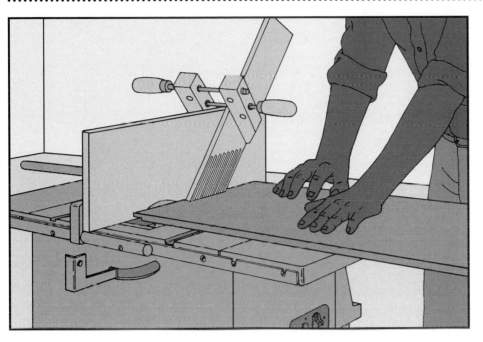

Rabbets.
◆ Install a dado head $\frac{1}{16}$ inch wider than the rabbet you plan to cut, and position the notched fence so the extra $\frac{1}{16}$ inch lies under the notch.
◆ Clamp a featherboard to the fence and position the workpiece underneath it *(page 13)*.
◆ Turn on the saw. Slowly push the board over the dado head, using a push stick as the edge of the board nearest you approaches the blades.

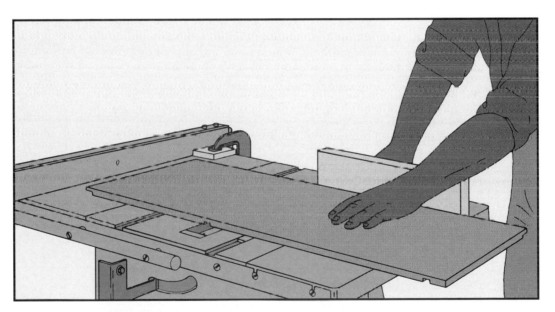

Dadoes.
◆ Fit the miter gauge with a 1-inch board to provide a broader surface for pushing the workpiece through the saw.
◆ Move the rip fence aside and clamp a wooden stop block to the table near the front of the saw, positioned to align the workpiece with the dado head.
◆ Place the board against the miter gauge, with its end against the stop block.
◆ Turn on the saw. While holding the board down with one hand, advance the miter fence and board with the other.

19

Over the course of time, cabinets may develop annoying ailments: Drawers stick, doors fit imperfectly, and shelves develop a wobble or sag. Most of these problems, however, are easily fixed.

Drawers: Some cabinets have drawers with grooved sides, which slide along cleats in the sides of the cabinet. In other styles the bottom edges of the drawer sides serve as runners that sit atop guides fastened to the cabinet; many wide drawers also have center runners and guides.

When a drawer refuses to slide freely, the problem is usually with the cleats or runners. If a worn cleat is the culprit, replace it *(page 24)*. Severely worn bottom runners require either building up with wood veneer *(page 22)* or replacement *(pages 22-23)*.

Drawer joints also loosen over time. Often you can reglue one loose joint without taking the drawer apart. But when the entire drawer is loose and rickety, disassemble and rebuild it *(page 25)*.

Doors: If a cabinet door binds either because it is warped or because the surrounding frame is twisted out of square, you can reshape the door through sanding or planing *(pages 29-30)*. Another remedy is to reposition the hinges slightly *(page 28)*.

Shelves: A major problem with shelves is their tendency to sag.

The solution can be as simple as flipping the shelf, although badly warped or cracked shelves should be replaced.

When a shelf wobbles or tips, a weakened support is usually to blame. You can rebuild shelf-pin holes when they are worn *(page 28)*, but all other types of support are best replaced.

Useful Renovations: Old cabinets can often be modified so that they suit new needs. You can remove the drawers in a cabinet, for example, and add interior partitions to support shelving *(pages 31-32)*. And with the addition of rails and supports, a cabinet that once held shelves can be converted to hold drawers *(page 33)*.

The Right Glue: Many of the following procedures call for gluing together wood components. To determine which glue to use in each case, consult page 37.

TOOLS

Hammer
Nail set
Wood planes
Utility knife
Try or combination
  square
Wood chisel

Mallet
C clamps
Electric drill
Carpenter's nippers
Small nail puller
Pipe clamps
Awl
Keyhole saw
Saber saw

MATERIALS

Candle or soap
Chalk
Sandpaper (60-,
  100-, 150-grit)
Wood veneer strips
Contact cement
Glue

Wood screws
Brads
Finger latch
Hardwood dowel
Lumber ($\frac{3}{4}$" and
  1 x 2)
Wood putty
Molding ($\frac{3}{4}$" square)
Plywood ($\frac{1}{2}$")

SAFETY TIPS

Protect your eyes with safety goggles when you are hammering, drilling, sawing, or working with power tools.

Cabinet trouble spots.

Shown at right are some cabinet elements that can cause problems. Doors—both flush and lipped—can bind from sagging or frame warpage; shelves bow; and drawer joints and guides (not visible here) wear.

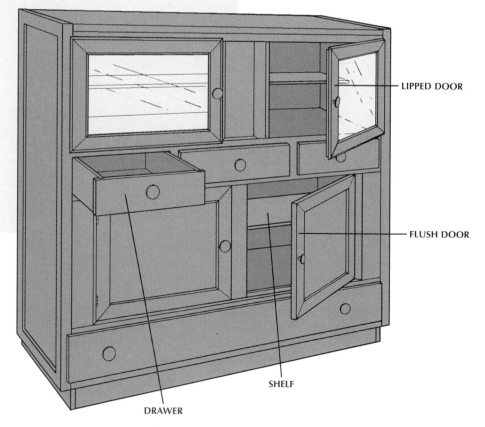

LIPPED DOOR

FLUSH DOOR

SHELF

DRAWER

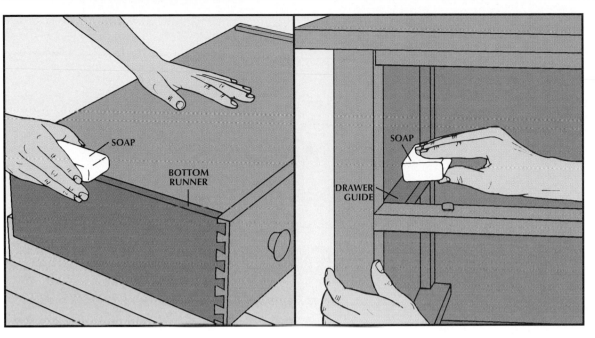

Lubricating surfaces.
Sticking drawers can run smoothly with a coat of soap or wax on runners and guides.
◆ Pull the drawer out of the cabinet and place it upside down on a work surface.

◆ Rub soap or a candle along the entire length of both drawer runners *(above, left)*. If there is a center runner, lubricate it also.
◆ Use a hammer and nail set to countersink protruding nailheads on the drawer guides, then coat

their sliding surfaces as you did the runners *(above, right)*.

For drawers that glide along side cleats and grooves, apply the lubricant along all surfaces of each cleat and groove.

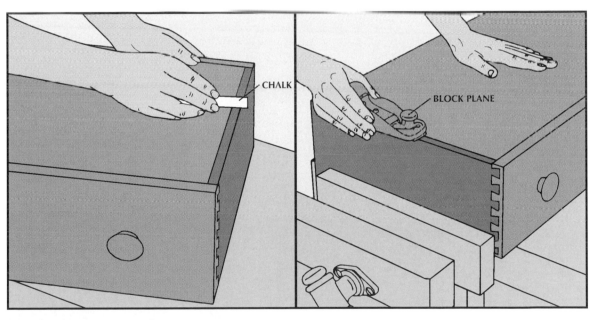

Shaving an uneven edge.
Where lubrication doesn't free a sticking drawer, wood may have swollen or warped. If the drawer has bottom runners, try the following technique:
◆ Invert the drawer on a work

surface, and rub chalk along the runners *(above, left)*.
◆ Return the drawer to the cabinet and slide it in and out several times, then inspect the chalked edges; the chalk will have rubbed off of any high

spots on the runners that are causing the drawer to stick.
◆ Plane or sand the high spots *(above, right)*, frequently testing the fit of the drawer to avoid removing more wood than necessary for smooth operation.

BUILDING UP A WORN DRAWER RUNNER

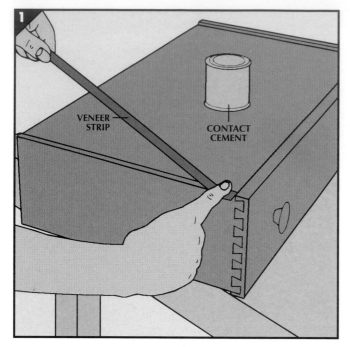

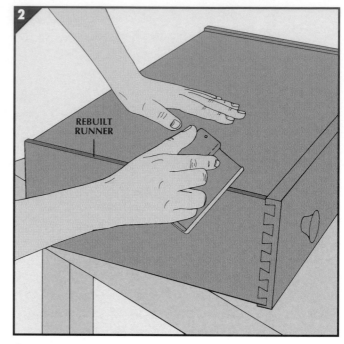

1. Attaching a veneer strip.

In addition to the glue-on veneer shown here, you may also use heat-bonding veneers, which are applied with a household iron.

◆ With 100-grit sandpaper, sand the runner smooth.
◆ Cut a veneer strip slightly longer than the runner.
◆ Brush a thin, even coat of contact cement on the runner and veneer. Allow about 5 minutes for the glue to dry; then, starting at one end *(above),* press the veneer firmly onto the runner, ensuring that the edges bond.
◆ Repeat the procedure to install a strip on the other runner, if necessary.

2. Trimming to fit.

◆ With a utility knife, trim any veneer that extends over the ends and sides of each runner.
◆ Lightly smooth the veneer strip along its edges with 100-grit sandpaper *(above).*
◆ Return the drawer to the cabinet and test the fit. If the runners are too high, sand them down. Add a second layer of veneer to runners that are still too low.
◆ Lubricate the rebuilt runners with soap or a candle.

REPLACING A RUNNER

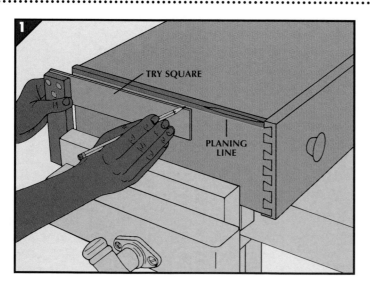

1. Drawing a planing line.

◆ Turn the drawer upside down and secure it with a workbench vise or between boards clamped to a worktable.
◆ With a try square or a combination square, draw a planing line on the drawer side just below the area of most wear *(left).*
◆ Measure and record the length, width, and depth to the planing line of the runner, taking the depth measurement where the runner is least worn.

2. Trimming a worn runner.

◆ Use a jack plane *(page 8)* to pare down a runner to the planing line *(right)*. Hold the plane level and maintain even pressure; take care not to nick the front of the drawer.

◆ Remove the part of the runner inaccessible to the plane with a wood chisel. Hold the chisel at an angle, beveled side down, and lightly tap the handle end with a mallet *(inset)*. Chisel the wood in thin layers down to the planing line.

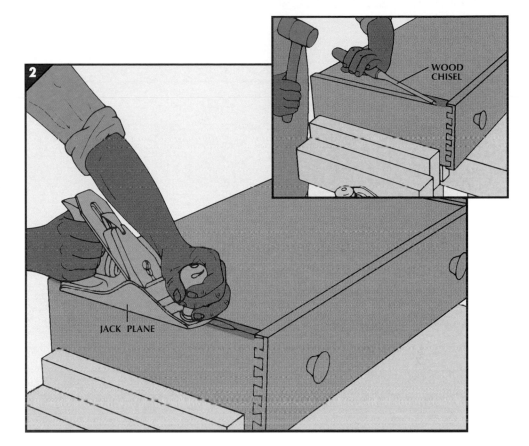

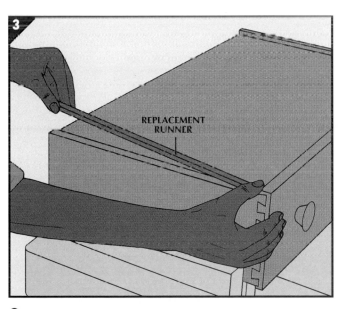

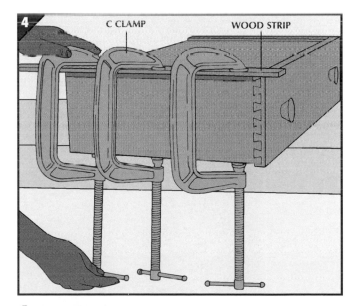

3. Installing the new runner.

◆ At a lumberyard specializing in millwork, have a piece of hardwood cut to the dimensions noted in Step 1.

◆ Spread a thin coat of glue on the new runner and the drawer side, and press the parts together *(above)*.

4. Securing the repair.

◆ Hold the new runner in place with C clamps, inserting a wood strip between clamps and runner to distribute the pressure. Tighten the clamps only enough to bring the two surfaces evenly together *(above)*.

◆ Wipe away excess glue with a clean, damp cloth.

◆ Wait for the glue to dry thoroughly, then test the drawer in the cabinet. Sand the new runner to fit with 100-grit sandpaper, then lubricate with soap or a candle.

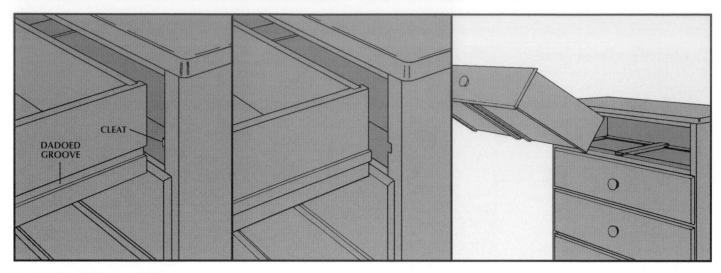

Replacing drawer cleats.

A cleat-and-groove assembly can easily be repaired if the cleat becomes worn. The drawer sides in the picture at left above are dadoed to fit over cleats attached to the cabinet frame. In the center picture, cleats attached to drawer sides slide in dadoes in the frame. In the third design, two cleats on the bottom of the drawer form a groove that slides on a cleat in the center of the frame, while the drawer sides rest atop the sides of the frame.

To replace a cleat, trace its outline, remove it, then cut and install a duplicate within the outline. Use glue and screws to attach a cleat to a frame; fasten a cleat to a drawer with glue only, so screwheads do not snag the drawer's contents.

Flipping a sagging drawer bottom.

Use this technique only for sagging bottoms that are structurally sound; replace split or broken bottoms with a piece of plywood.
◆ With carpenter's nippers or a small nail puller, remove the brads that fasten the bottom to the drawer back. If the drawer has small glue blocks that join the bottom to the drawer front or sides, detach the blocks with a chisel.
◆ Slide the bottom from the dadoes in the drawer sides. If the bottom fits into a dado in the drawer back, the drawer will have to be disassembled (page 25).
◆ Turn the bottom over and reassemble the drawer with brads and glue blocks.

REBUILDING A DRAWER

1. Disassembling the pieces.
◆ Pull the drawer out of the cabinet and set it on a work surface. Remove the drawer bottom *(opposite, bottom)*.
◆ If the drawer front is dovetailed to the sides and the back is dadoed into the sides *(right)*, loosen the joints by tapping on the sides inside each corner. Place a block of wood against the side of the drawer at the front corner, and strike the block sharply with a mallet or hammer. Repeat the procedure at the back corner, then on the opposite side, tapping the corners alternately so that all four joints come apart gradually.

For a drawer having sides dadoed rather than dovetailed into the front *(inset)*, tap on the drawer front at the corners, then tap the sides at the back corners. Separate the back and front from the sides.

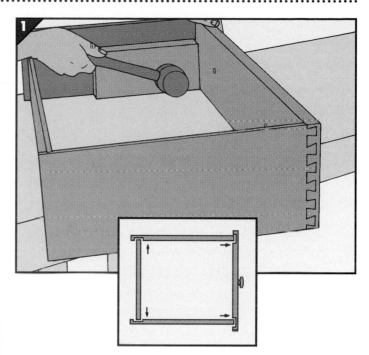

2. Reassembling the drawer.
◆ Scrape off the dried glue from the joints, taking care not to damage the fingers of dovetails.
◆ Spread a thin coat of glue on the joints.
◆ Attach the sides first to the front of the drawer, then to the back. Tap the joints tightly together.
◆ Slide the drawer bottom into the grooves in the sides.
◆ Attach pipe clamps to the drawer at the reglued joints *(left)*, padding the clamp jaws if they contact the drawer front. Tighten the clamps only enough to bring the gluing surfaces in contact.
◆ To ensure that the drawer is clamped square, measure diagonally from the front right corner to the back left corner, then from the front left corner to the back right corner. If these two measurements are not equal, adjust the fit of the clamps to make them so.
◆ With a clean, damp cloth, wipe away any glue beading out of the joints. Release the clamps once the glue sets.

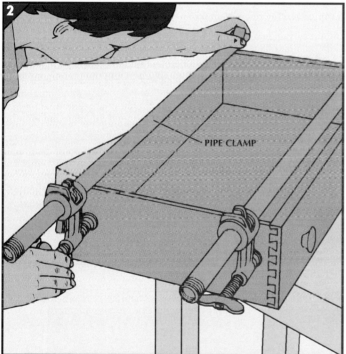

PIPE CLAMP

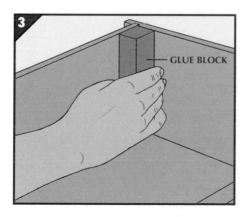

GLUE BLOCK

3. Reinforcing the repair.
If the drawer is used to store heavy items, glue blocks can help the drawer front withstand the stress of repeated openings.
◆ Cut four wood blocks to fit inside the drawer.
◆ Apply a thin coat of glue to an end and two sides of each block and the inside corners of the drawer. Press the blocks into each corner *(left)*, rubbing them up and down several times to remove any air bubbles.
◆ Do not use the drawer until the glue has dried.

DIAGNOSING AND SOLVING DOOR PROBLEMS

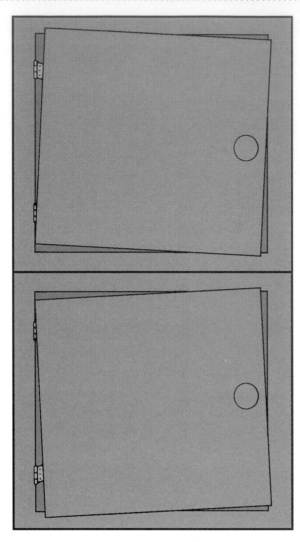

What to look for and how to fix it.

Examine the door for warping and rubbed areas. If the tight spots are hard to see, chalk the door edges, then open and close the door several times. The chalk will transfer to the frame where the door is sticking. Alternatively, insert a sheet of paper between the edge of a flush door and the cabinet; the paper will move freely around the door except at the sticking points.

Minor rubbing is often remedied simply by tightening the hinge screws; if the screw holes are worn, install longer screws or rebuild the holes *(page 28)*. More serious rubbing, especially if it is caused by doors tilted as shown in these exaggerated diagrams, may require adjustment of the hinges. To fix a door that binds near the lower hinge *(left, top)*, shim that hinge *(below)* and deepen the mortise of the upper hinge with a chisel *(opposite)*; a door that pinches near the top hinge *(left, bottom)* calls for the opposite treatment. In cases where hinge adjustment fails to fix the problem, the last resort is to reshape the door by sanding or planing *(pages 29-30)*.

To hide a noticeable warp, you can either install a finger latch or throw the hinges *(page 28)*.

SHIMMING A HINGE

Fitting the shim.

◆ Open the door and wedge a piece of wood or cardboard under the bottom corner to prevent the door from sagging.
◆ Remove the screws that mount the hinge to the cabinet frame.
◆ Slip a thin piece of cardboard behind the detached hinge. Use an awl to scribe the outline of the hinge leaf on the cardboard and to pierce it at the screw hole

locations *(right)*.
◆ Remove the shim from behind the hinge and trim it about $\frac{1}{16}$ inch smaller than the outline.
◆ Slide the shim into the unoccupied mortise; reattach the hinge to the cabinet.
◆ Pull out the wedge and open and close the door. If it continues to stick, add another shim to bring the hinge flush with the wood surface, or deepen the other hinge's mortise *(opposite)*.

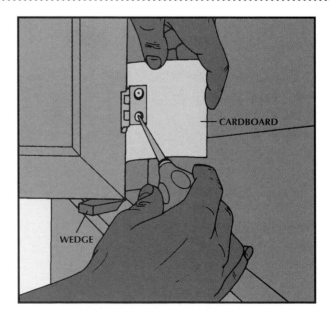

CARDBOARD

WEDGE

DEEPENING A HINGE MORTISE

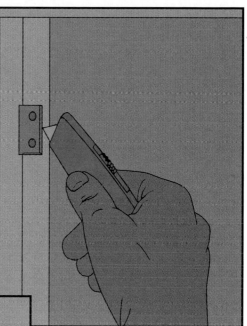

1. Preparing the mortise.
◆ Remove the door from the cabinet frame.
◆ Score the mortise perimeter with a utility knife to a depth of $\frac{1}{16}$ inch *(right)*. The scored line serves as a boundary for cutting the mortise with a chisel in the next step.

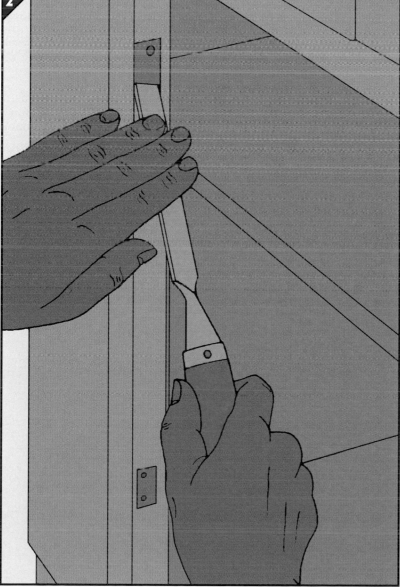

2. Chiseling the mortise.
◆ Using a wood chisel with the beveled edge facing down, shave a thin, even layer of wood out of the mortise *(left)*. Only light hand pressure is necessary for the chisel to remove the wood.
◆ Remount the door. If the hinge leaf does not sit evenly in the new mortise, the mortise surface is not flat; even it out with the chisel.
◆ Check the fit of the door. If it is necessary, deepen the mortise further.

ACCOMMODATING A WARPED DOOR

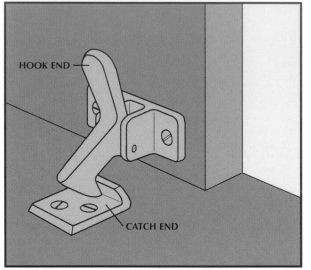

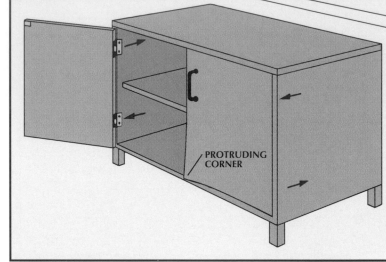

Installing a latch.

A finger latch can hide a warp of a few eighths of an inch on a double door. For a greater warp, move the hinges *(right)*.

◆ With the screws provided, mount the hook end of the latch on the lower inside corner of the cabinet door at the manufacturer's specified height.

◆ Mount the catch end on the cabinet bottom across from the hook end, at a distance from the edge equal to the manufacturer's specification plus the displacement caused by the warp.

Repositioning the hinges.

This technique, called throwing the hinges, requires enlarging hinge mortises, a process similar to deepening them *(page 27)*.

◆ Measure the displacement at the protruding corner. The hinge closest to the corner will move inward by half this distance, the other hinge outward an equal amount.

◆ Hold the hinge that moves inward in its new position, and trace its outline against the cabi-

net. Scribe the outline with a utility knife, and enlarge the mortise with a chisel.

◆ Fill the old screw holes *(below)*, drill new ones, and remount the hinges.

If there is one warped door in a set of double doors, divide the displacement equally among all four hinges and move them as shown by the arrows above. When both doors are warped, deal with each one individually.

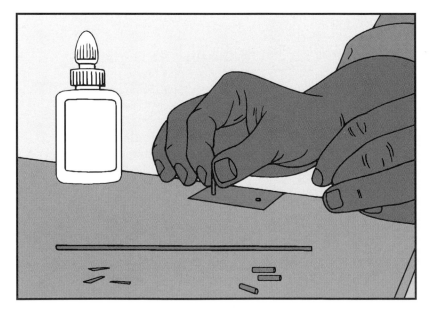

Filling in a hole.

To plug a screw hole, as well as a worn shelf-pin hole *(page 51)*, use the following procedure:

◆ Cut a hardwood dowel into sections as long as the hole is deep.

◆ Splinter the dowel sections lengthwise with a chisel or utility knife.

◆ Fill the hole with glue, then push as many splinters as possible into it, tapping the splinters with a hammer to plug the hole tight. Wipe off excess glue.

◆ If the hole is to be reused, drill a new pilot hole after the glue dries.

A Drill Bit for Accurate Pilot Holes

A device called a self-centering bit *(photograph)* has a guide with a beveled end that automatically centers the tip of the bit in a hinge hole *(left)*, giving consistently more accurate results than the traditional method of marking the holes with an awl. To use the bit, place the tip of the guide in the hole and begin drilling. As the bit advances, the guide retracts; when you withdraw the bit, a spring restores the guide to its original position.

GUIDE

SPRING

SELF-CENTERING BIT

FREEING A STICKY DOOR

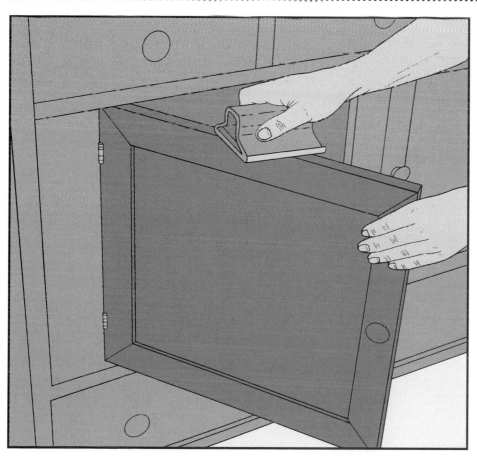

Sanding down a high area.

If the door sticks on the bottom, or close to its hinges, dismount it before sanding. Use a plane instead of sandpaper to remove more than $\frac{1}{16}$ inch of wood *(page 30)*.

◆ To locate binding points, rub chalk along the door edges, then open and close the door several times and look for the areas where the chalk has rubbed off.

◆ Sand the tight spots with 100-grit sandpaper wrapped around a sanding block *(left)*. Test the fit of the door often to prevent oversanding.

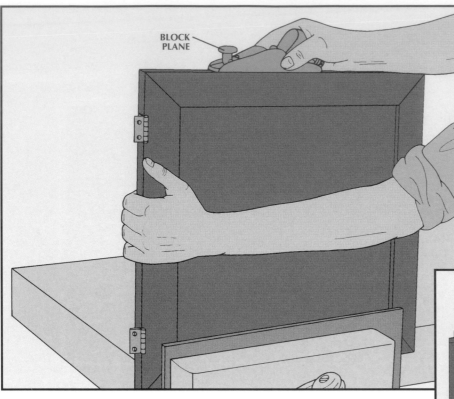

BLOCK
PLANE

Planing a binding edge.

◆ Place the door in a vise, protecting its finish with wood or cardboard.
◆ With a block or jack plane *(page 8)*, shave the door along the grain *(left)*. Work from the corners to the center to prevent splintering of the side rails. Keep even pressure on the plane and use long shearing strokes. Remove wood sparingly, remounting the door often to test its fit.

For lipped doors, use a rabbet plane *(inset)*, which is made for trimming notched edges.

A QUICK FIX FOR SHELVES

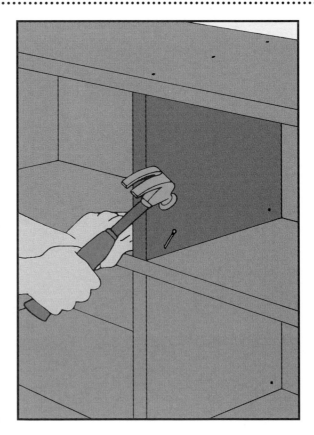

Reinforcing a sagging shelf.

Install a support not only under the shelf that sags but under all shelves below it; otherwise the sag will be transferred to the next lower shelf. Screws will serve instead of nails to fasten the braces, provided you countersink the heads.
◆ At an end of the cabinet or bookcase, measure the distance between shelves, starting at the bottom and ending with the sagging shelf. From $\frac{3}{4}$-inch-thick lumber as wide as the shelf is deep, cut supports as long as the measured distances.
◆ Beginning at the bottom of the cabinet and proceeding one support at a time *(right)*, center a support between shelves, then butt-nail it in place through the upper shelf and toenail it to the shelf below.

SUBSTITUTING SHELVES FOR DRAWERS

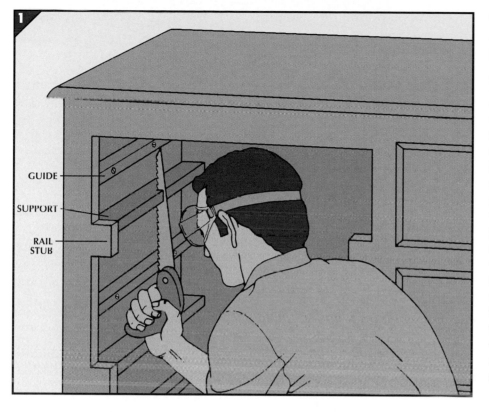

GUIDE

SUPPORT

RAIL
STUB

1. Gutting the interior.

◆ Remove the drawers and cut the horizontal rails from the face frame just inside drawer guides and supports, leaving short rail stubs that will be cut off later.

◆ If a support piece is glued to the front and back of the cabinet as well as to the side, cut it in half with a key-hole saw *(left)*. Take out all nails and screws holding the guides and supports in place.

◆ Break the glue bonds by tapping the guides and supports with a hammer, and pull out the pieces.

◆ Cut the rail stubs as close to the edges of the face frame as you can without scratching it. Using first 60-grit then 100- and 150-grit sandpaper, sand the cut ends flush.

◆ Fill with wood putty any cavities left after sanding, let the putty dry, and sand the surface smooth.

2. Fastening partition cleats.

Two cleats made from $\frac{3}{4}$-inch-square molding—one fastened to the back of the cabinet *(above)*, one to the front—hold the partition in place. Add as many partitions as necessary, each mounted behind a stile in the face frame, to keep the shelf length less than 32 inches.

◆ Cut the cleats to the interior height of the cabinet.

◆ To position the back cleat, use a combination square and a straight board to transfer the locations of the top and bottom corners at the front of the opening to the back of the cabinet as shown in the inset. Then draw a vertical line $\frac{1}{2}$ inch from these marks *(dotted line)*.

◆ Secure the cleat along the line with glue and screws.

◆ Mount the front cleat inside the face of the cabinet, $\frac{1}{2}$ inch away from the opening.

3. Installing the partition.

◆ Cut a partition from $\frac{1}{2}$-inch plywood to the cabinet interior's height and depth. If the partition does not fit through the opening, saw it in half horizontally and mount the halves separately.

◆ While holding the partition in place against the cleats *(left)*, drill at least four pilot holes for mounting screws in each cleat. Space the holes evenly on a line $\frac{3}{8}$ inch from the front and back edges of the partition.

◆ Remove the partition and spread glue on the drilled faces of the cleats.

◆ Return the partition to the cabinet and screw it into place.

4. Putting in a bottom.

◆ Cut 1-by-1 side cleats to the depth of the cabinet, and a front cleat that is $1\frac{1}{2}$ inches shorter than the cabinet's interior length.

◆ Draw level lines on the side, partition, and front, then fasten the cleats along the lines with glue and screws.

◆ Cut a bottom from $\frac{1}{2}$-inch plywood.

◆ Drill pilot holes for mounting screws, apply glue to the top of each cleat, and screw the shelf to the cleats.

◆ Install adjustable shelves *(pages 50-51)* and fit the cabinet with a door *(pages 87-88)*.

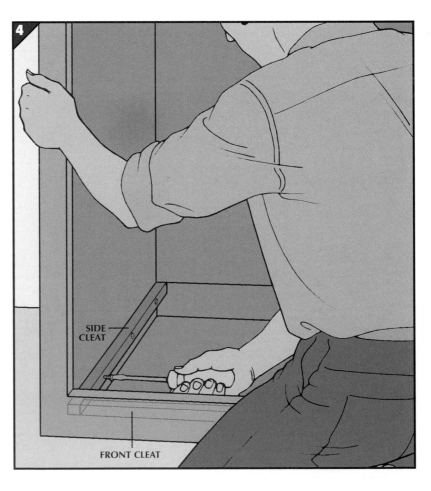

SIDE
CLEAT

FRONT CLEAT

SWITCHING TO DRAWERS FROM SHELVES

1. Clearing the space.

◆ To remove shelves glued into dadoes, use a saber saw fitted with a flush-cutting blade to cut a V to the back of the shelf. If the shelf extends through more than one section of the cabinet, make V cuts in each section, then saw lengthwise along the middle of the shelf to connect the Vs *(right)*.

◆ Tap the top and bottom of the remaining shelf pieces with a hammer to loosen the glue, then gently work them free.

◆ Where you have cut shelves that run through more than one section, install a partition between the sections *(pages 31-32)*.

To remove a shelf mounted on cleats, remove any nails or screws and then tap the shelf from below to break the glue bond; pry it off. Take the nails or screws out of the cleats, tap them to break the glue bond, and remove them also. Use carpenter's nippers to remove protruding nail or screw tips.

2. Installing drawer rails.

◆ From 1-by-2 lumber, cut rails to fit the face frame. With a paint scraper, clean varnish or paint from the face frame's edges where the rails will fit.

◆ Cut a pair of spacers to fit under the lowest rail and place them under the rail at each end for support. Then drill counterbored pilot holes into the cabinet stiles for toescrews through the top of the rail, $\frac{1}{2}$ inch from each end.

◆ Apply glue to the ends of the rail and screw the rail in place.

◆ Install the next higher rail, reusing the spacers for support as you drill pilot holes.

◆ After the glue dries, toe-screw each rail's bottom to the stiles.

Build drawers for the cabinet and install them *(pages 72-77)*.

Shelves for Every Purpose

Adding shelves along a wall is perhaps the easiest way to increase storage space or to display collections of books, sports trophies, and treasured souvenirs, items that seem invariably to overflow the space allotted to them. The options are numerous, from utility shelves supported by a couple of modest braces to freestanding units like the one shown in the closeup at right.

Planning a Project   36

Cutting Wood Efficiently
Nails versus Screws
Glues for Joining Wood

Simple, All-Purpose Shelving   38

A Single Shelf on Metal Braces
Hanging Shelves on Standards
A Range of Bracket Systems
Easy-to-Assemble Freestanding Shelves

A Shelf on Sturdy Brackets   43

Making and Mounting the Shelf

Floating Shelves   46

Hanging the Shelves

Shelving for a Wall   50

A Variety of Shelf Supports
Rectangular Shelves along a Wall
Triangular Shelves in a Corner

A shelf supported by a flush clip →

Shelves consisting of boards supported by brackets fastened to a wall are simple to plan for. Once you settle on the length, depth, and number of the shelves, you need only buy boards of the correct dimensions and enough brackets to support them *(pages 38-49)*.

But when shelves take the form of a cabinet—a structure with a top, a back, and sides—you need to consider carefully in advance the kind of wood to use and how the pieces will be joined together in a durable, attractive piece of furniture.

Planning the Pieces: For simplicity and economy, the shelves and cabinets on pages 50 to 55 and in Chapter 3 are made from high-quality plywood and trimmed with soft-wood boards and moldings *(pages 120-123)*. To minimize waste when cutting plywood pieces, make a cutting diagram *(right)*. Start with a piece of graph paper and draw a 4- by 8-inch rectangle on it to represent a standard, 4- by 8-foot, sheet of plywood.

Then, using the same scale, cut pieces from another sheet of graph paper to represent each piece of plywood needed for your project. Arrange the pieces efficiently on the rectangle and outline them in pencil. Transfer your plan to a sheet of plywood, leaving margins between the pieces at least as wide as your saw-blade kerf. As a precaution, remeasure after each cut before you saw the next one.

Strong Joints: Pieces may be joined with nails or screws; there are pros and cons for each *(box, opposite)*. Neither, however, should be used without glue. When combined with nails or screws, glue can form a joint so strong that the wood will break before the joint will separate.

Whenever you use glue, remember to wipe off any excess immediately; where glue dries, it will clog the wood's pores and prevent it from taking a stain.

Cutting wood efficiently.

The cutting diagram below shows the best way to cut a sheet of plywood for a two-shelf version of the corner unit shown on pages 53 to 55. Whenever possible, preserve the plywood's factory edges and plan cuts so that waste *(gray)* comes from the interior of the sheet. A further consideration is grain. Arrange the pieces so that, for example, the grain runs in the same direction on both ends of a cabinet.

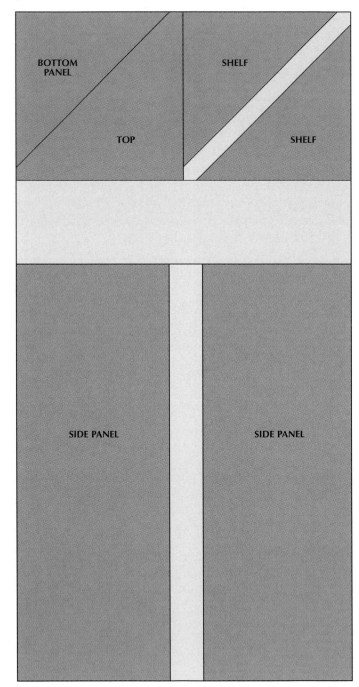

COMMON NAIL

FINISHING NAIL

DRY-WALL SCREW

FLAT-HEAD WOOD SCREW

NAILS VERSUS SCREWS

Nails, the most common fasteners, are quick, easy, and inexpensive. Especially when they are reinforced with glue, nails offer adequate strength for virtually any cabinet or shelf unit. Of the many types of nails sold, only two are needed for most shelf and cabinet construction: common nails and finishing nails. Common nails have large heads and work well in places where they will not be seen. Finishing nails have small heads that can be countersunk and concealed; they serve best on exterior parts where an unblemished surface is desired.

Screws cost more and take more time to install than nails but have better holding power and are necessary where extra strength is needed. Use them also to attach parts of a structure you may later want to disassemble. Both flat-head wood screws and dry-wall screws are commonly employed in woodworking because they are easily countersunk beneath a wood surface and concealed.

All screws require the drilling of pilot, or starter, holes for the threads; in some cases, the top of the hole must be enlarged once for the unthreaded part of the screw and again to countersink the screwhead. These two- or three-tiered screw holes can be made with regular drill bits boring one hole after another, or with a special combination bit that does the entire job in a single step. If screws still prove difficult to drive, rub soap or wax on the threads to lubricate them.

Glues for Joining Wood

Type	Characteristics
Polyvinyl glue (white)	For general woodworking. Strong bond; dries clear and colorless. Not waterproof; does not sand well. Nontoxic.
Carpenter's or wood glue (yellow)	For general woodworking. Strong bond; dries opaque. Not waterproof; better sanding qualities than polyvinyl glue. Nontoxic.
Resorcinol	Bonds in wet, humid areas. Strong, permanent bond. Dries dark; waterproof. Must be mixed; can be sanded. Toxic.
Contact cement	For dissimilar materials. Bonds on contact; water-resistant. Use in well-ventilated area. Toxicity varies with type.
Epoxy	Good for joints that can't be clamped. Strong, permanent bond. Must be mixed; waterproof. Toxic. Wear gloves and use in well-ventilated area.

TRICKS OF THE TRADE

A Glue Applicator

Keeping the glue for your project at the ready is easy with a setup like the one shown here. Pour glue into the bottle provided and set it upside down in the base so that the adhesive remains near the top of the bottle, ready to flow. A special tip on the bottle applies a smooth and even bead of glue to any surface.

Simple, All-Purpose Shelving

With the right hardware, adding to your shelf space can be a simple job, no matter what your shelving needs. A single, stationary hanging shelf is usually supported by braces, attached directly to the wall; angle-iron braces *(below)* or versions made of molded metal will take heavy loads. If you want several hanging shelves that you can move or remove easily, support them with brackets that fit into upright standards installed on the wall *(pages 40-41)*. Still other kinds of hardware allow you to put together freestanding shelves with a minimum of effort *(page 42)*.

Secure Support: Braces or standards used for wall-mounted shelves should be spaced 20 to 32 inches apart, depending on the load the shelves will carry. If the supports are separated by more than 32 inches, wood shelving may sag under its own weight. Do not extend the ends of a shelf more than 8 inches beyond the outside supports; longer ends may cause bowing and decrease stability.

If you are hanging shelves on walls that are hollow, attach the braces or standards to studs whenever it is possible; an electronic stud finder will locate these framing members accurately. Since most studs are about 16 inches apart, a support that is attached to every other stud will work for most loads. For other types of walls, or when studs are not available, secure the supports with the appropriate fasteners *(page 119)*.

Careful Alignment: When you position a shelf either horizontally or vertically, do not rely on visual judgment; always use a level. Wall, ceiling, and floor lines are seldom straight, even in new homes.

 TOOLS

Electronic stud finder
Carpenter's level
Awl
Electric drill

Tape measure
Combination square
Screwdriver
Hex wrench

 **MATERIALS**

Braces
Wood for shelves
Wall fasteners
Wood screws
Standards, brackets, and hardware

Corner clips
Corner braces
Round-head brass pins ($\frac{3}{4}$")

 **SAFETY TIPS**

Wear safety goggles when drilling or hammering to protect against eye injury by woodchips or nails.

A SINGLE SHELF ON METAL BRACES

1. Aligning the first brace.
◆ After deciding where to mount the shelf, position the first brace: Hold a level vertically against the brace and the wall, and adjust the position until the air bubbles in the level's end vials are centered.

◆ With an awl, scratch circles through the screw holes of the brace.

◆ Remove the brace and drill pilot holes in the wall. Make sure the drill bit is precisely centered in the marked circles; even a small error can throw off the alignment.

◆ Attach the brace to the wall with the appropriate fastener.

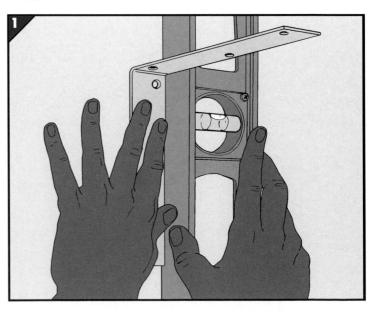

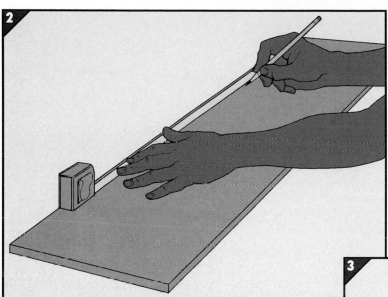

2. Positioning the other braces.

◆ If the shelf needs only two braces, decide on the amount of overhang you want at each end. Measuring in from each end, mark the shelf on its underside to indicate where the braces will be centered.

◆ If the shelf requires more than two braces, mark for the end braces the same way, then measure the distance between these positions *(left)* and divide the measurement by the number of additional braces you intend to use plus one. This figure will provide an equal distance from brace to brace.

◆ Mark off these distances to indicate the centers of the intermediary braces.

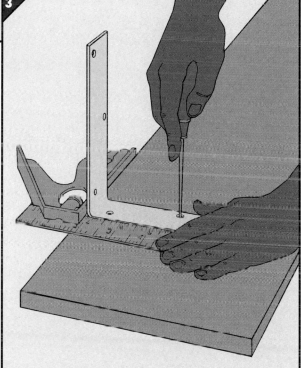

3. Setting the second brace.

◆ Center the second brace on one of the marked positions on the shelf (except where the brace already attached to the wall will be fastened).

◆ Square the brace along the back edge of the shelf by fitting it against a combination square *(right)*.

◆ Mark the screw holes with an awl, drill pilot holes, and attach the brace to the shelf with wood screws.

◆ Attach any other braces in the same way, centering them on the positions marked on the underside of the shelf.

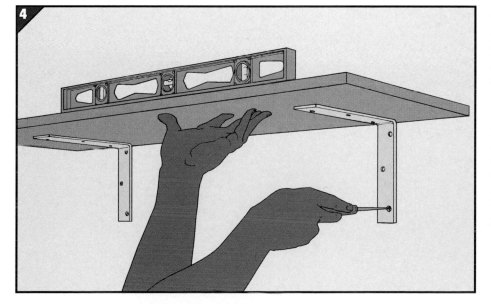

4. Leveling the shelf.

◆ Rest the shelf on the brace already fastened to the wall. Center the brace on the mark made for it on the shelf.

◆ Level the shelf and, with an awl, mark the wall through the screw holes in the other braces *(left)*.

◆ Remove the shelf and drill pilot or anchor holes in the wall.

◆ Replace the shelf and fasten the braces to the wall.

◆ Drill pilot holes in the shelf through the holes in the brace first fastened to the wall. Drive in wood screws.

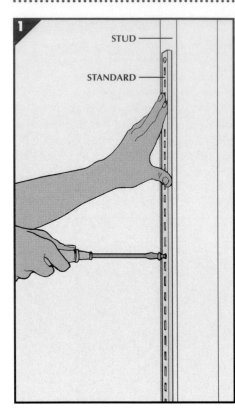

STUD

STANDARD

1. Positioning the first standard.

◆ Determine the location of the standards as in Step 2, page 39, with at
least one of them centered on a stud.
Lightly mark the location of the standards on the wall.

◆ Place one of the end standards
against the wall, top end up. Mark one
fastener hole—the center one if there
are more than two. Drill a pilot or anchor hole and drive in an appropriate
fastener to hold the standard to the
wall—but do not tighten the fastener.

2. Attaching the standard.

◆ With a level, align the standard
vertically.

◆ Mark the positions of the other
fastener holes and, if necessary,
swing the standard aside when
you drill the pilot or anchor holes.
Center the drill bit precisely.

◆ Holding a level against the
standard as a final check on
alignment, attach the remaining
fasteners *(right)*.

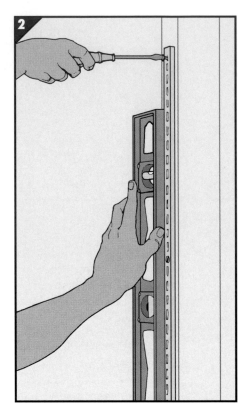

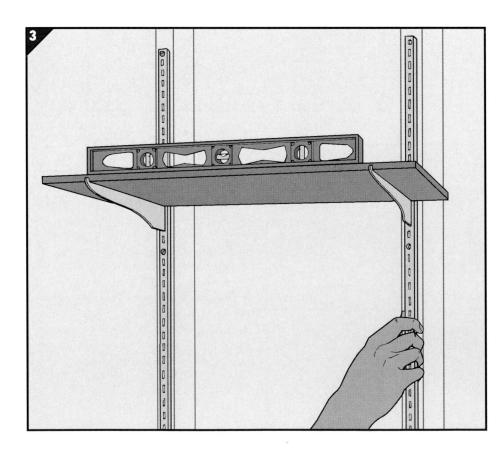

3. Hanging the shelf.

◆ Insert a shelf bracket in the mounted standard, then fit another bracket
into the corresponding holes of a second standard.

◆ Place the second standard against
the wall, centering it on the mark
made for it, and place the shelf on top
of the brackets. Level the shelf.

◆ Mark the top and bottom of the second standard on the wall; remove the
shelf and attach the second standard
as described in Steps 1 and 2.

◆ If more than two standards are required, repeat Step 3 for each.

A RANGE OF BRACKET SYSTEMS

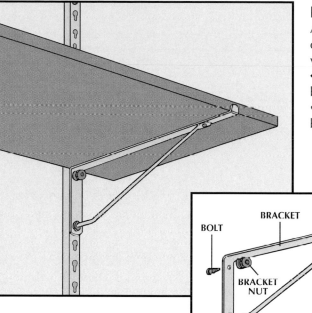

Keyhole.
A triangular design enables brackets of this type to support weights that are very heavy.
◆ Slip the bolts that come with the brackets into the standards' holes.
◆ Press the bolts down and tighten the bracket nuts.

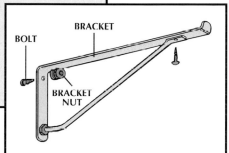

Tracked.
This slotted metal standard is fitted with sliding inserts equipped with a bolt and flat nut.
◆ To attach a bracket, press an insert into the track of the standard. The top of the insert must be at shelf level minus the thickness of the bracket.
◆ Tighten the bolt with a hex wrench *(inset)* until the nut grips the standard.
◆ Slip the spade pin at the end of the bracket sideways into the standard's slot. Turn and fit the bracket into the groove on the face of the insert.

Carved wood.
These decorative brackets are hooked over screws driven into their standards.
◆ To attach a bracket, partially drive a screw into the standard at the desired shelf height minus the distance from the top of the bracket to the small, metal-lined hole on the bracket's inner surface *(inset)*.
◆ Fit the hole over the projecting screwhead.

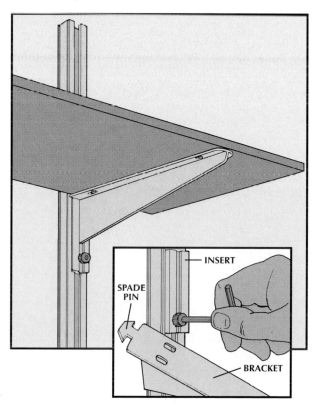

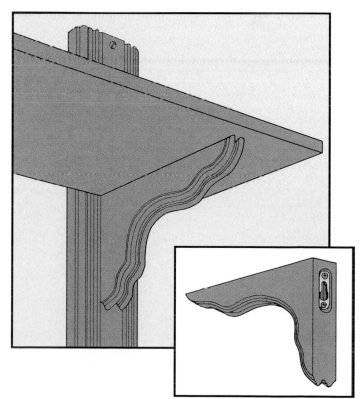

EASY-TO-ASSEMBLE FREESTANDING SHELVES

With corner clips *(top right)* or corner braces *(bottom right)*, you can quickly assemble freestanding shelf units in almost any configuration you choose. The brass-plated clips are available in two sizes: $\frac{3}{4}$ inch for 1-inch softwood boards and $\frac{5}{8}$ inch for laminated particle board. Their cross, L, and T shapes fit any right-angle joints. When figuring how many of each clip to buy, remember those for the back, as well.

Whether the unit's boards are sawed by you or the lumberyard, make sure the cuts are square. Before fastening the clips, assemble the boards on the floor to check for fit, then sand and finish them before reassembly. Fasten the clips with 16-gauge round-head brass pins, $\frac{3}{4}$ inch long. Drive the pins through the small holes on the front of the clips, not the larger ones on the sides, which result from the manufacturing process.

Small, $1\frac{1}{2}$-inch angle irons, called corner braces, hold shelves together less conspicuously. If you are using 1-inch boards, fasten the braces with $\frac{3}{4}$-inch, No. 6 flat-head wood screws, driven into $\frac{1}{16}$-inch-wide pilot holes. Make sure that screws driven from opposite sides of a board will not collide, and assemble the pieces in such an order that boards fixed in place leave you room to drill holes and drive screws for later boards.

Corner braces do not provide much rigidity; you may nail on a $\frac{1}{4}$-inch plywood back for stability.

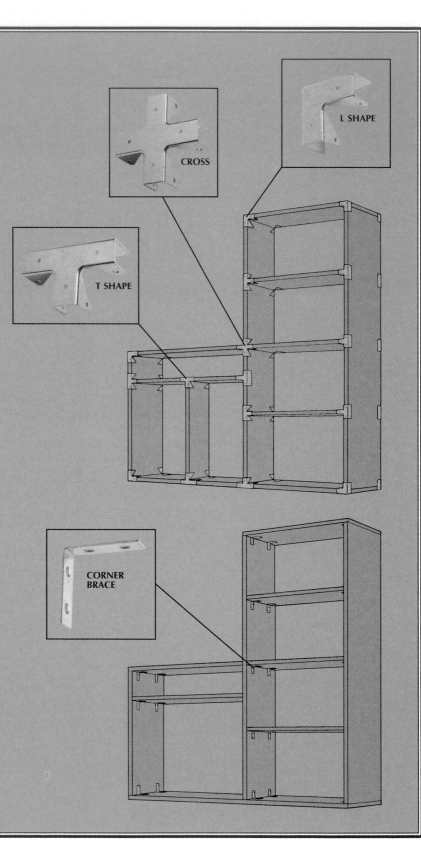

CROSS

L SHAPE

T SHAPE

CORNER BRACE

A Shelf on Sturdy Brackets

You can tailor this handsome shelf to your individual space needs, making it as little as 36 inches long or—providing you use an additional bracket every 4 feet—extending its length to 12 feet.

Customizing Your Plans: All of the components for one shelf, including the curved brackets, can be cut from a single length of nominal 1-by-12 lumber *(page 121)*. First, determine the desired finished shelf length and add 1 foot for each bracket. Select an appropriate board and have your lumber dealer cut off 1-foot-long pieces from one end for the brackets. From the remaining piece, have the dealer ripcut a 2-inch-wide strip for the cleat. The dowel plugs can be purchased ready made from a hardware store or they can be cut at home with a backsaw and miter box.

Cut the curved brackets with a saber saw. You can shape the brackets more fancifully to a design of your own; just keep the length of each leg the same as in the pattern in Step 1 on page 44, and be sure that no part of the design is too narrow to support the load—a width of 1 inch is the minimum necessary.

TOOLS

Flexible or French curve
Pair of C clamps
Saber saw
Sanding block
Electric drill and bits
Electronic stud finder
Carpenter's level

MATERIALS

1 x 12
Sandpaper (60-grit)
Dowel plugs
Glue *(page 37)*
Wood screws (2" No. 10)

SAFETY TIPS

Goggles offer protection for your eyes when you are drilling or sawing.

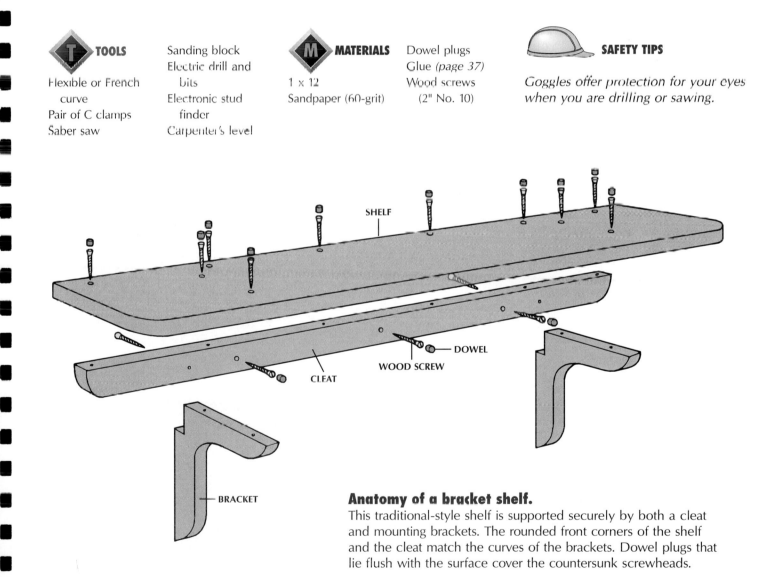

SHELF

DOWEL

WOOD SCREW

CLEAT

BRACKET

Anatomy of a bracket shelf.
This traditional-style shelf is supported securely by both a cleat and mounting brackets. The rounded front corners of the shelf and the cleat match the curves of the brackets. Dowel plugs that lie flush with the surface cover the countersunk screwheads.

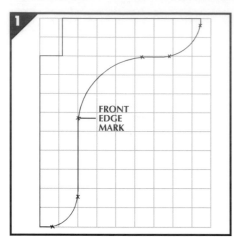

1. Creating the bracket pattern.

◆ Make a grid of 1-inch squares on a 9- by 11-inch piece of lightweight cardboard or heavy paper.
◆ Draw a notch in one corner of the grid, and two lines for the bracket's top and back edges. Then mark the points where the front edge of your design crosses the grid. Using a flexible or French curve, smoothly connect the marks. Cut out the pattern.
◆ Position the bracket pattern on one of the 1-foot pieces of wood, making sure that the upward sweep of the pattern runs in the same direction as the wood's grain. Trace around the pattern.
◆ Transfer the pattern for the other brackets in the same way.

2. Cutting the brackets.

◆ Position one bracket piece on a work surface, with the notch of the pattern overhanging the edge. Clamp the board in place and cut out the notch with a saber saw.
◆ Then move and reclamp the piece so the curved pattern overhangs the work surface, and cut out the bracket *(right)*.
◆ Clamp and cut additional brackets in the same way.
◆ Sand the curves of the brackets *(pages 108-109)*.

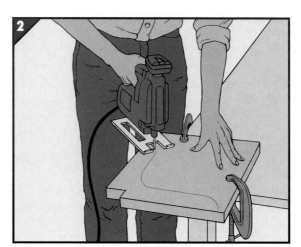

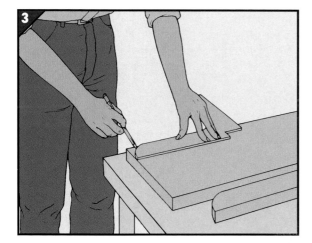

3. Rounding the corners.

◆ Lay the mounting cleat flat and pencil a mark that is 2 inches from each end on its 2-inch surface.
◆ Place the pattern on the cleat so that the inside edge of the pattern aligns with one long side of the cleat and the curved tip rests at the pencil mark. Trace the curve onto the wood.

◆ Repeat at the other end of the cleat, turning the pattern over and marking both curves on the same side of the board.
◆ Clamp the cleat and cut the corners with a saber saw.
◆ Lay the curved tip of the bracket pattern onto the edge of each end of the shelf, and trace and cut rounded corners *(left)*.
◆ Sand the cut edges.

4. Counterboring screw holes.

◆ Lightly pencil a line $\frac{1}{2}$ inch from and parallel to the shelf's long edge on the side opposite the rounded corners. Mark across it 3 inches from each end and in between at equal intervals of about 12 inches, depending on the board's length.
◆ Then draw lines across the width of the board 12 inches from each end, and make perpendicular marks across the lines 2 inches and 7 inches from the marked edge.
◆ Raise the shelf from the work surface with scraps of wood, and with a $\frac{3}{8}$-inch twist bit bore $\frac{1}{2}$-inch-deep holes at each spot where the lines and marks intersect. Then, with a $\frac{3}{16}$-inch bit, bore through the wood at each hole.

Alternatively, use a combination bit to create each hole.

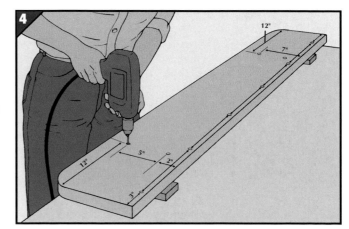

5. Leveling the cleat.

◆ Measure 10 inches from each end of the cleat and mark the center of its broad face.

◆ Using a ruler, draw a line across the wall where you want the shelf.

◆ With an electronic stud finder locate and mark the studs behind this section of wall.

◆ Hold the cleat's top edge flush with the penciled line and its marked side facing the wall.

◆ Center the cleat on the stud lines, level it, and mark the stud lines on the cleat *(right)*.

◆ Mark the center of the cleat's face at each stud line. As in Step 4, drill counterbored holes through the wood at the marks. Turn the cleat over and drill similar holes at the 10-inch marks on the other side.

6. Joining the pieces.

◆ On a work surface, align the cleat so that its back edge is flush with the bottom surface of the shelf. (The back of the cleat is the side that has only two counterbored holes.) The shelf should overhang the cleat by 2 inches at each end.

◆ Clamp the pieces together at both ends using wood to protect the surfaces.

◆ With a $\frac{3}{16}$-inch twist bit, drill pilot holes in the top of the cleat through the holes in the shelf *(left)*.

◆ Unclamp the pieces and then apply glue to the top surface of the cleat.

◆ Line the holes up, clamp the pieces back together, and secure with screws. Remove the clamps.

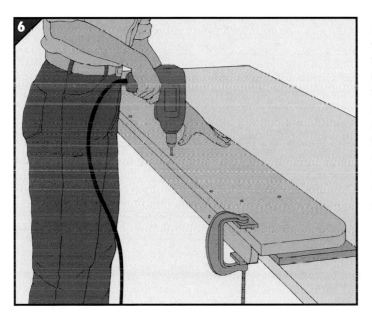

7. Attaching the mounting brackets.

◆ Clamp the shelf facedown and center the notch in one bracket on the holes in the mounting cleat and the shelf.

◆ With a $\frac{3}{16}$-inch twist bit, drill a pilot hole through the cleat into the bracket *(right)*, and secure with a screw. Repeat with other brackets.

◆ Unclamp the shelf, turn it right side up, and drill pilot holes into each bracket through the shelf holes. Secure with screws.

◆ Unscrew the pieces, apply glue to the notch and top of each bracket, then reattach.

◆ Sand and finish the shelf as desired *(pages 108-117)*, and mount the shelf to the studs through the screw holes in the cleat.

◆ Cover the holes in the cleat and the shelf with dowel plugs, then sand and finish them.

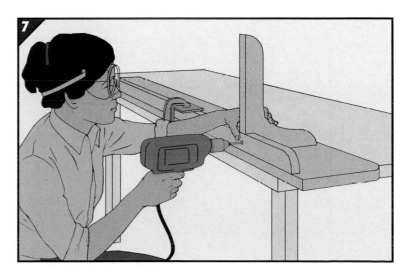

Floating Shelves

These shelves, suspended freely, offer a spare, uncluttered look. Their supports are invisible but sturdy: Each shelf is held aloft by two steel rods sunk into both the wall studs and the back of the shelf.

What You Need: The shelves can be arranged in virtually any pattern on a wallboard or wood-frame plaster wall where rods can be driven at least 3 inches into the studs. The rods also must extend nearly halfway into the shelves. For strength, use threaded or plain $\frac{3}{8}$-inch steel rods that have been cut to measure at a hardware store.

Each shelf must be at least 20 inches long (to cross two studs) and no more than 40 inches long, and may project up to a foot beyond each stud. To hold the rods, the shelves must be solid hardwood or softwood boards at least $1\frac{3}{4}$ inches thick. For stability, they should be no deeper than 10 inches.

To make sure that each shelf sits properly against the wall, plane the wood accurately. If you have it planed by the lumberyard, check each piece with a square to see if its top surface and back edge meet at a 90-degree angle.

To produce level shelves, make sure that all holes are drilled in a perfectly straight line. A drill guide helps to keep the bit from swerving *(pages 48-49).*

Working on the Wall: Because the rods must be sunk into the exact centers of studs, it is important to work along a level, horizontal line so that your measurements remain constant. You can mark stud positions and the horizontal guideline with chalk or by tacking string to the wall. Chalk is quick to apply but may be difficult to remove. To test your wall, make a chalk mark in an inconspicuous place, then wash it away. If a stain remains, either use string and tacks or plan to repaint or repaper the wall after you have installed the rods.

Additional minor repairs and touch-up painting will be needed to conceal the exploratory holes that verify the location of each stud center. After drilling into the studs, but before mounting the shelves on the wall, sand and finish the shelves as desired *(pages 108-117).*

> ⚠️ **CAUTION** *When drilling into walls, beware of pipes and electric cables. If you hit pipe or cable, stop immediately and call a plumber or an electrician.*

TOOLS

Tape measure	Cat's paw
Chalk line	Electric drill with $\frac{3}{8}$"
Electronic	bit
stud finder	Drill guide
Carpenter's level	Vise
Hammer	Awl

MATERIALS

Hard- or softwood	Steel rods ($\frac{3}{8}$")
boards (at least	Spackling
$1\frac{3}{4}$" thick)	compound
Graph paper	Sandpaper (150-grit)
Drafting tape	Hardwood stick
Finishing nails	(6"-8" x 1" x $\frac{1}{2}$")
($1\frac{1}{2}$")	Dowels ($\frac{3}{8}$")

SAFETY TIPS

Goggles help to protect eyes from flying nails or woodchips when you are hammering or drilling.

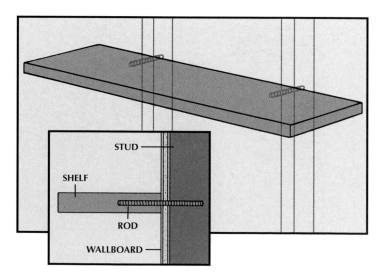

Concealed support.
Holes drilled into wall studs support the steel rods that anchor these shelves. The rods extend deeply into both the studs and the shelves, as seen here in cross section *(inset).*

HANGING THE SHELVES

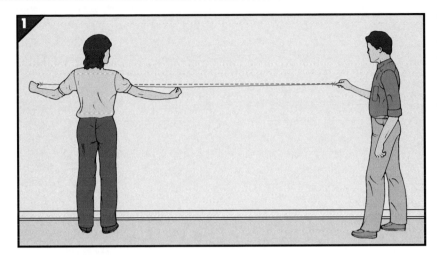

1. Snapping a chalk line.
◆ With a tape measure and chalk, mark two points at the left and right ends of the planned shelf area.
◆ Have a helper hold the end of a chalk line at one mark (or tack the end at that mark).
◆ Stretch the line to the opposite mark, hold it taut, pluck the line out from the wall *(left)*, then let it go.

2. Locating the studs.
◆ Working from left to right along the chalked line with an electronic stud finder, find and mark the location of each stud in the shelf area.
◆ Using the chalk line as a plumb bob, have a helper hold one end so that the string crosses over the stud location mark.
◆ Pull the chalk line's string taut and snap a vertical chalked line *(left)*.
◆ Repeat at each stud.

VERTICAL CHALKED LINE

HORIZONTAL CHALKED LINE

STUD LOCATION MARK

3. Planning the design.
◆ Make a scale plan of the wall on graph paper, drawing in the stud lines and the proposed shelves.
◆ Using the plan as a guide, measure up from the floor along two studs and mark where the top of the first shelf will lie.
◆ Have a helper hold a level just above the marks, and attach a strip of drafting tape to the wall; align the tape's top edge with the bottom edge of the level *(left)* and run the tape the length of the shelf.
◆ Repeat at each shelf location.

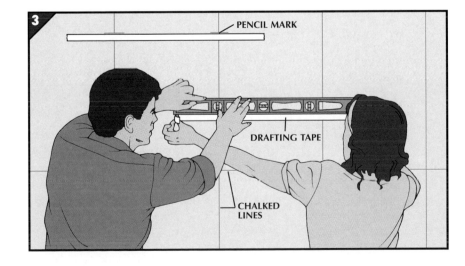

PENCIL MARK

DRAFTING TAPE

CHALKED LINES

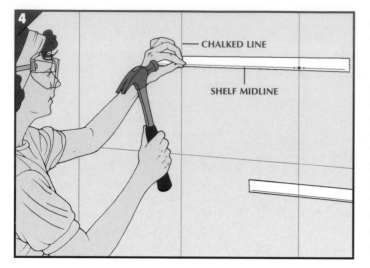

4. Making starter holes.

◆ Measuring from the top of each piece of drafting tape, make a mark on the tape to represent the midline of the shelf's thickness. At the mark, using a level as a straight-edge, pencil a horizontal line across the tape. With pencil, continue each vertical chalked line across the tape.

◆ At the intersecting pencil lines, tap a $1\frac{1}{2}$-inch finishing nail through the wallboard just until you feel it enter wood. Repeat to the left and right of that place, using the nail to locate the edges of the stud. Mark the midpoint between the edges to indicate the stud's center.

◆ With the same nail, make a $\frac{1}{2}$-inch-deep starter hole at each stud center point. If you hit a nail already in the stud, extract it with a cat's paw.

◆ Remove the pieces of tape.

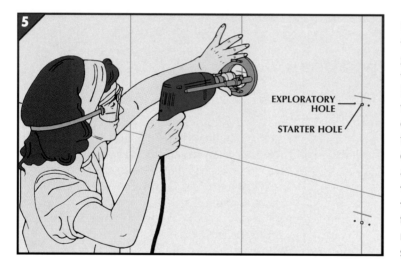

5. Drilling holes at stud centers.

◆ Fit a drill with a $\frac{3}{8}$-inch twist bit and a drill guide set to drill holes $3\frac{1}{2}$ inches deep.

◆ Drill into the wall at each starter hole, holding the drill guide's base against the wall with one hand while pushing the drill with the other *(left)*. If you have extracted a nail from the wallboard near one of the starter holes, drill at that hole instead, then use a level to adjust the height of the shelf's other hole.

◆ Insert a $\frac{3}{8}$-inch steel rod into each hole.

◆ Clean the wall, apply spackling compound to the exploratory holes, and let it dry overnight. Smooth the compound with 150-grit sandpaper, then paint over it.

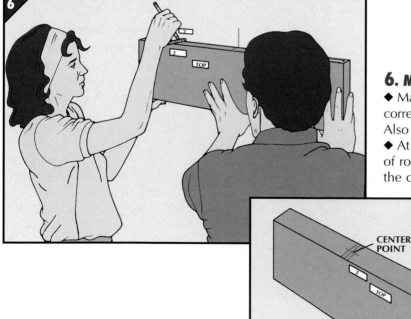

6. Marking the shelf for drilling.

◆ Mark each shelf and its location on the wall with corresponding numbers written on drafting tape. Also label each shelf's top surface and back edge.

◆ At the wall, mark the center point between a pair of rods, then mark the center of the back edge of the corresponding shelf.

◆ Have a helper hold the shelf flat against the wall, aligning the center mark on the back edge with the mark on the wall. Draw lines along the rods' sides onto the back edge of the shelf *(left)*.

◆ Locate the center point between each line pair with perpendicular lines *(inset)*.

◆ Similarly mark the remaining shelves.

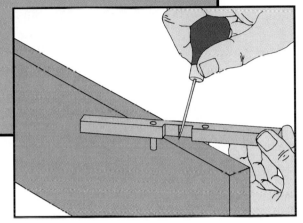

A Board-Edge Centering Jig

To make a floating shelf level requires precisely centering the holes in the shelf's back edge. The jig shown here makes quick work of finding exact center. To make the jig, cut a 1-inch-wide and $\frac{1}{4}$-inch-deep recess on a piece of hardwood about 6 to 8 inches long, 1 inch wide, and $\frac{1}{2}$ inch thick. Mark or scribe a line along the center of the recess and drill a hole on either side of the recess 1 inch from the centerline. Insert a dowel in each hole, flush with one side and extending $\frac{1}{2}$ inch on the other.

Place the jig on the board edge and twist it until the dowels fit snugly up against either side of the board. Then, mark the board at the jig's centerline as shown at right. Drill at the mark.

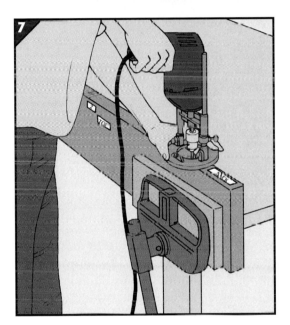

7. Drilling the holes in the shelf.

◆ Secure a shelf, marked edge upward, in a vise, using two pieces of scrap wood to protect the shelf's surfaces.
◆ With a $\frac{3}{8}$-inch bit and the drill guide still set for $3\frac{1}{2}$ inches, drill straight through each marked center point, using an occasional pumping motion to draw out woodchips.
◆ Drill identical holes in the remaining shelves.

8. Setting the shelves.

◆ Keeping them in numbered order, sand and finish the shelves.
◆ After the shelves have dried, fit each one onto the wall, carefully placing first one hole over a rod, then the other.
◆ Push the shelf back until it is flush with the wall.

Built-in shelves that blend into the design of a room provide a fairly simple yet attractive way of creating additional space that can be used for storage or display.

Functional and Versatile: The design of these shelves depends on your choice of supports, where the unit will be located, and what it will hold. Arranged between side panels, shelves can rest on simple cleats or pins, or on movable clips in recessed or surface-mounted standards *(below and opposite).*

Shelving can be built to any height or length, but to support books or other heavy objects, make individual shelves no longer than 32 inches. Divide longer shelving into sections with vertical partitions for support.

When deciding on depth, consider that hardbound and paper-back books fit well on 8-inch shelves, while encyclopedias and art books need 10 to 12 inches. Using full-width boards of the desired depth saves having to make difficult lengthwise cuts. Size triangular corner shelves to display small objects and collectibles or to house audio equipment and TV sets.

A Perfect Fit: For shelves that blend into the woodwork, remove baseboard and other trim before beginning construction. To do so, score the joint between baseboard and wall with a utility knife, protect the wall with cardboard or a wood block, and work the baseboard free with a pry bar.

Before reinstalling the old baseboard, measure and cut it to abut the shelf base. Painting the unit to match the baseboard and trim completes the custom-built effect.

Construction Options: Make rectangular shelf units along a wall from 1-by-8, 1-by-10, or 1-by-12 clear lumber *(page 121).* Corner shelves require hardwood plywood and 1-by-4 boards. Cover exposed plywood edges with veneer or with solid edging strips *(page 55).*

A table saw makes quick work of the two units described here, but you also can use a hand-held circular saw *(pages 10-11).* Before nailing, coat the surfaces of all joints with glue *(page 37).* As an alternative to nails, dry-wall screws driven flush with the surface through counterbored pilot holes offer added strength *(page 37).*

 TOOLS

Utility knife	Pliers
Pry bar	Carpenter's level
Hammer	Electronic stud
Screwdriver	finder
Electric drill and bits	Combination square
Table saw or	Backsaw and miter
circular saw	box
File	Nail set

 **MATERIALS**

1 x 3s	Common nails (3")
1 x 4s	Finishing nails ($1\frac{1}{2}$")
1 x 8s, 1 x 10s,	Dowels ($\frac{3}{8}$" or
1 x 12s for	larger)
shelves	Metal spade or
Hardwood plywood	bracket pins
($\frac{3}{4}$")	Slotted standards
Glue	Gusset or flush
Dry-wall screws	clips
Moldings ($\frac{3}{4}$" square	Brads (1")
and $\frac{3}{8}$" x $1\frac{1}{4}$")	Wood putty

SAFETY TIPS

To protect eyes from flying nails or woodchips, wear safety goggles when nailing, drilling, or sawing.

A VARIETY OF SHELF SUPPORTS

Wood cleats.
Solid wood offers strong support and can be finished to match the shelves.
◆ Cut strips of $\frac{3}{4}$-inch molding $\frac{1}{2}$ inch shorter than the depth of the shelf, and saw the front edges to a 45-degree angle.
◆ Nail or screw pairs of cleats to the side panels so their tops are level and at an equal height from the base.
◆ For extra stability, drive small finishing nails through the shelf into the cleats.

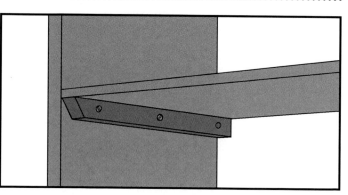

Dowels and pins.

Short lengths of wood dowel or metal spade or bracket pins make economical supports for shelves that do not carry heavy weight. For a secure fit, drill the side panel holes the same diameter as the dowels or pins. Drill shelf-support holes at the same height on both sides to keep the shelf level.

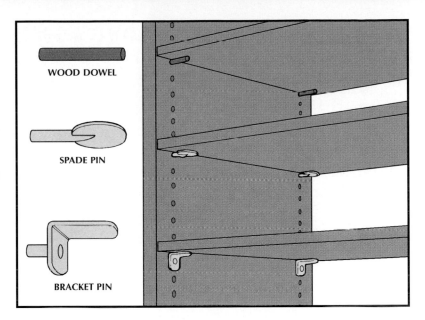

WOOD DOWEL

SPADE PIN

BRACKET PIN

TRICKS OF THE TRADE

A Hole-Spacing Jig

A level shelf that doesn't wobble requires four shelf support holes, all of which are bored at the same height above the base of a shelf unit. To make the job of drilling such holes simpler, build the jig that is shown here. It consists of a 1-by-3 that has evenly spaced holes along the centerline, which is extended onto both ends of the board to aid alignment. The holes are the same diameter as the shelf supports that you plan to use, as is a 1-inch length of dowel that is glued in the hole at one end of the jig so that it protrudes $\frac{1}{4}$ inch.

Use the jig first with the dowel pointing up, as shown in the illustration below. To extend the line of holes turn the jig over, insert the dowel in the last hole made, and continue drilling.

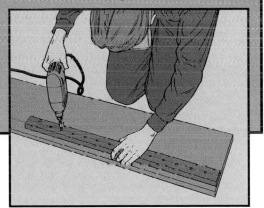

DOWEL

Clips and standards.

Slotted standards can be screwed or nailed to the side of a bookcase or cabinet, or dadoed in for a neat, flush fit.

◆ Cut the standards to length, and smooth the edges with a file.

◆ With pliers, install one gusset or flush clip in the center slot of each standard.

◆ Mount the standards with screws, aligning them with a level.

◆ Insert additional clips according to the shelf heights that are desired.

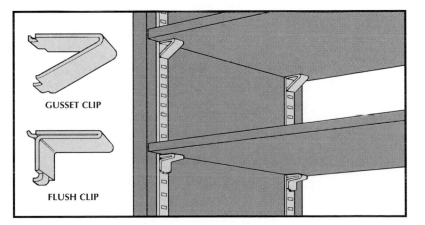

GUSSET CLIP

FLUSH CLIP

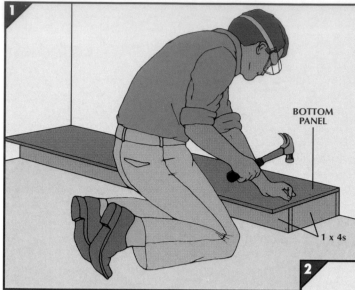

BOTTOM PANEL

1 x 4s

1. Constructing the base.

◆ From 1-by-4 lumber, cut two pieces $\frac{3}{4}$ inch shorter than the width of the finished shelf unit, for a corner unit, or $1\frac{1}{2}$ inches shorter, for a freestanding one, and two pieces $4\frac{1}{2}$ inches shorter than the depth.

◆ Nail the 1-by-4 pieces into a rectangular base, long pieces overlapping short ones at the corners.

◆ Locate the studs in the adjoining wall and fasten the base to the studs with 3-inch nails.

◆ For the bottom panel, cut a 1-inch board to the width of the base and to the depth of the finished unit.

◆ Nail the bottom panel on top of the base with $1\frac{1}{2}$-inch finishing nails *(left)*, flush with the sides and back with a 3-inch overhang at the front.

2. Attaching the sides and top.

◆ For shelves with both sides exposed, cut two side panels to the desired height and depth with a 3- by $3\frac{1}{2}$-inch notch in each to fit the base. For a corner unit, cut the unexposed side $4\frac{1}{4}$ inches shorter than the other, without a notch.

◆ To recess the shelf standards, cut a dado that is 1 inch from the front and back edges of each side panel, with the blade set to the width and depth of the standards *(pages 16-17)*.

◆ Nail the side panels to the base along the notch and bottom, $\frac{3}{8}$ inch from the edge. For a corner unit, toenail the bottom of the shorter panel to the top of the base.

◆ To make the top, cut a board to the width and depth of the finished unit.

◆ Nail the top to the side panels *(right)*, making sure the edges and sides are flush.

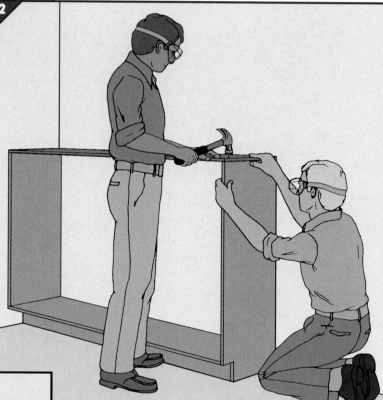

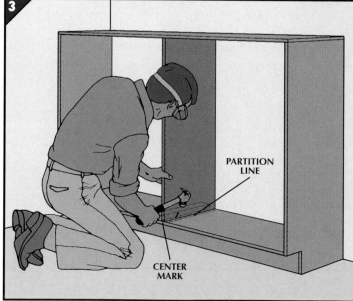

PARTITION LINE

CENTER MARK

3. Installing a partition.

◆ Cut a board of the same depth as the unit to the inside measurement between the top and the bottom panel. If recessing shelf standards into the partition, offset the dadoes $\frac{1}{2}$ inch on opposite sides of the partition so that mounting screws will not meet.

◆ Mark the base's center. With a combination square, scribe a line from front to back of the base $\frac{3}{8}$ inch to one side of the center. Temporarily nail a block of wood along the line to steady the partition as you toenail it.

◆ Hold the partition against the block and toenail it to the bottom panel with $1\frac{1}{2}$-inch finishing nails every 3 inches *(left)*; remove the block and toenail the partition from the other side.

◆ Align the partition vertically with a level. Nail through the top of the unit into the partition to secure it.

4. Fitting the shelves.

◆ Screw standards into dadoes you may have cut in the side panels earlier, or surface mount the standards as follows:

◆ Rest a standard on the base 1 inch from the back. With a level, align it vertically and attach it with screws. Screw another standard $1\frac{1}{2}$ inches from the front. Install the remaining standards in the same way, offsetting those on opposite sides of the partition by $\frac{1}{2}$ inch so the screws do not meet.

◆ Measure the distance between the standards at the bottom panel, then insert shelf clips in the standards at the desired height for each shelf. Measure at each set of clips.

◆ Cut shelves that are $\frac{1}{8}$ inch shorter than the shortest of the measurements and set them on the clips.

TRIANGULAR SHELVES IN A CORNER

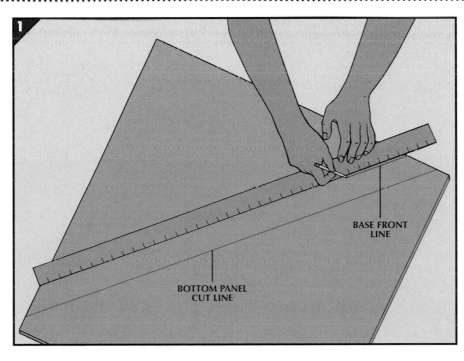

BASE FRONT LINE

BOTTOM PANEL CUT LINE

1. Laying out dimensions.

◆ Cut a square of $\frac{3}{4}$-inch hardwood plywood with sides about 2 inches longer than the planned sides of the unit.

◆ Measuring from one corner, mark the proposed depth of the shelves on adjacent sides of the square. Using a straightedge, join the marks with a cut line for the bottom panel.

◆ To make a template for the front and sides of the base, draw a base front line parallel to the first line, 3 inches closer to the corner (left).

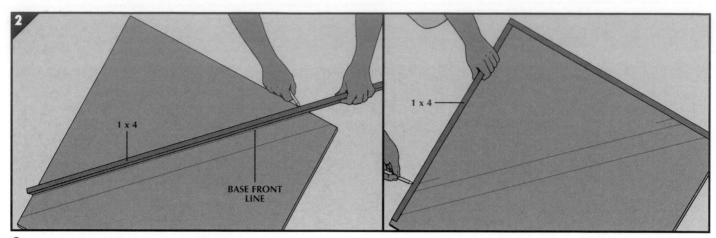

2. Cutting the base front and sides.

◆ To make the front, place a 1-by-4 on edge along the inside of the base front line. Pencil a short line on the plywood at each end of the 1-by-4. Mark both sides of the 1-by-4 where it meets each plywood edge *(above, left)*.

◆ Using a combination square, transfer the marks to the top of the 1-by-4. Draw a line between the marks and cut along the line with a table saw or a with a backsaw *(page 9)* and miter box.

◆ For the base sides, set two pieces of 1-by-4 on the plywood, their ends butted at the corner *(above, right)*. Mark the boards where they meet the short lines. With a combination square, make 45-degree cut lines and saw the base sides to length.

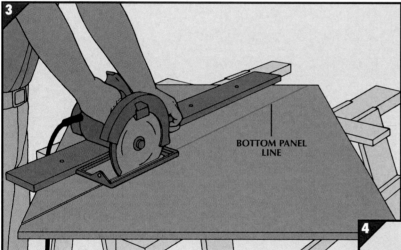

3. Forming the base.

◆ Nail the 1-by-4 base front and base side pieces together with $1\frac{1}{2}$-inch finishing nails to form a triangular base.

◆ Locate the wall studs and fasten the assembly to them with 3-inch nails.

◆ Cut the plywood along the bottom panel line, using a straightedge to guide the saw *(left)*.

◆ Attach the bottom panel to the base with $1\frac{1}{2}$-inch finishing nails spaced 4 inches apart.

4. Making beveled sides.

◆ Measure the depth of the bottom panel from the corner of the wall *(right)*. Transfer these measurements to plywood for the side panels, subtracting $\frac{3}{4}$ inch on one of the panels for a butted joint at the corner. Also mark the panels for the height of the unit.

◆ Cut the panels to height with a table saw or circular saw set for a square cut. Then tilt the blade to a 45-degree angle and bevel-cut the panels to the correct depth. For recessed shelf standards, cut dadoes 1 inch from each panel's front edge and 2 inches from the back *(page 17)*.

◆ Nail the panels together at the corner with $1\frac{1}{2}$-inch finishing nails.

◆ Set the side panel assembly on the base and toenail it to the bottom panel. Then nail the side panels through the wall to the studs.

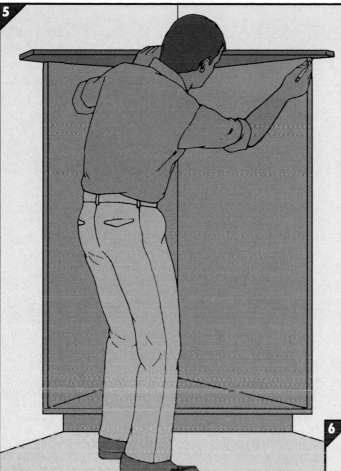

5. Attaching the top.

◆ Set the remaining part of the plywood square on top of the side panel assembly, its square corner tight against the wall. Mark the underside of the top where it meets the edges of the side panels *(left)* and join the marks with a pencil line.

◆ Cut along the line, then nail the top to the side panels.

◆ Fasten the shelf standards to the side panels and insert shelf clips at the desired heights *(page 53, Step 4)*.

◆ To fit a shelf, slip a square piece of plywood between the side panels, corner first, and set it on shelf clips. Mark the plywood where it meets the front edges of the side panels and draw a line $\frac{1}{4}$ inch inside the marks.

◆ Cut along the line; then, with the leftover piece of plywood, make another shelf.

6. Finishing the edges.

◆ Cut $\frac{3}{8}$- by $1\frac{1}{4}$-inch molding to fit the exposed plywood edge at the top of the unit, then the sides. Cut shelf edging to fit between the side pieces.

◆ Start 1-inch brads in the molding at 6-inch intervals.

◆ Spread a thin coat of glue on the plywood edges. Then press the molding against the glue and drive the brads into the edges. Countersink the brads with a nail set.

◆ Wipe off any excess glue with a damp paper towel, and let the glue set for an hour.

◆ Fill nail holes and any gaps with wood putty, then sand and finish the unit *(pages 108-117)*.

Cabinets and Wall Systems

In essence, cabinets are nothing more than boxes, carefully built and fitted with one or more partitions, shelves, drawers, or doors. This chapter explains not only how to plan and build virtually any cabinet, from a stand-alone bookcase to a suite of units for an entire wall, but also how to customize the furniture you build with a variety of door and drawer styles.

Planning a Cabinet   58
Diagrams Drawn to Scale

Building the Cabinet Carcass   62
Assembling the Box

Framing the Cabinet Front   66
Two Ways to Build a Face Frame
Assembling a Frame with Wood Biscuits
Joints Made with Dowels

Making and Installing Drawers   72
The Basic Drawer
Cutting a Double-Dado Joint
Installing Drawer Glides
A Drawer with Wood Runners
Adding a False Front to a Flush Drawer

Making and Hanging Cabinet Doors   78
Different Ways to Fit Doors
Two Styles of Doors
The Frame for a Frame-and-Panel Door
Shaping the Panel
Cabinet Hinges
Catches and Latches
Hinging Overlapping Doors
Hinging Inset Doors
Mortising Hinges on Overlapping Doors
Mortising Hinges on Inset Doors

A Versatile Wall System   90

A Compact Computer Center   92
Making the Desktop
A Printer Platform
Mounting the Desk

A Bookcase Accompaniment   97
Bridging between Modules

An Adaptation for a Television   99
A Sliding, Rotating Shelf
Joining Cabinet Modules

Marking a door for a hinge mortise →

Planning a Cabinet

A cabinet consists of a plywood carcass—a box with a top, bottom, back, sides, and partitions. Exposed plywood edges are concealed by boards assembled into a structure called a face frame *(page 66)*. You can add drawers *(page 72)* and doors *(page 78)* to suit your needs.

General Rules: The design of a cabinet is largely a matter of individual taste; doors, drawers, and shelves can be arranged in virtually any configuration. Even so, a few rules of thumb apply.

You must be able to tilt a floor-to-ceiling cabinet upright without scraping the ceiling; a diagonal measured across the front of the cabinet must be at least 1 inch less than the ceiling height.

Cabinets generally should be no deeper than 24 inches. Drawers are usually no more than 24 inches

wide; doors wider than 20 inches tend to sag on their hinges. To prevent their drooping, shelves should not exceed 32 inches in width without intermediate supports.

Drawing a Plan: Detailed sketches help you make design decisions in advance, such as the type of joints that will be used *(page 16)*, the positions of shelves, the exact sizes of drawers and doors, and the way the doors will open and close.

Graph paper with eight divisions per inch simplifies the drawing of sketches. You'll need several, showing views of the outside of the cabinet from every vantage point: front, back, top, bottom, and sides. In addition, any box within the basic box—such as a drawer—requires its own drawings.

Make additional drawings, like the ones shown on pages 60 and 61,

for interior parts or for those that are too small to be drawn accurately on the external views. In these drawings, let each square on the graph paper represent $\frac{1}{8}$ inch or $\frac{1}{4}$ inch. These drawings, called sections, focus on such details as joint construction and the way drawers and doors fit into the structure.

Choose the Materials: To work out the measurements on both the exterior and sectional drawings, you need to decide where you will use plywood, which can be cut to any width, and where lumber, which comes in standard dimensions *(page 121)*. These details will dictate the items on a comprehensive materials list. Choosing the grade and finish of the wood *(pages 122-125)* can be left for later, but the wood's width and thickness must be shown on the drawings *(opposite)*.

Anatomy of a cabinet.

A cabinet rests on a base made from $\frac{3}{4}$-inch plywood or from unwarped 1-by-4s or 1-by-6s. It consists of a frame made with butt joints at the corners, as shown here, or with 45-degree miters. Crosspieces called spreaders, no more than 16 inches apart, reinforce the frame. Screwing strips at the ends allow for anchoring the cabinet to the base, which is built 6 inches narrower and 3 inches shallower than the cabinet to leave a kick space around the exposed sides.

Cabinet sides are dadoed to accommodate the cabinet bottom; generally, sides extend $\frac{3}{4}$ inch below it. A $\frac{1}{4}$-inch-deep rabbet *(page 16)* in the sides accommodates

the back. Rabbeted into the upper ends of the sides and dadoed for a center partition are two top supports, each cut 4 inches wide from plywood or made with 1-by-4 lumber. The top, usually of plywood framed in 1-by-2 parting bead, is screwed to the supports. It overhangs the cabinet on the exposed sides to a depth that depends on the design of the cabinet and whether decorative molding and trim will be added *(pages 104-107)*.

In a cabinet with drawers, like this one, the center partition and sides are dadoed for drawer supports that are the same size as the top supports and whose edges are concealed by rails in the face frame.

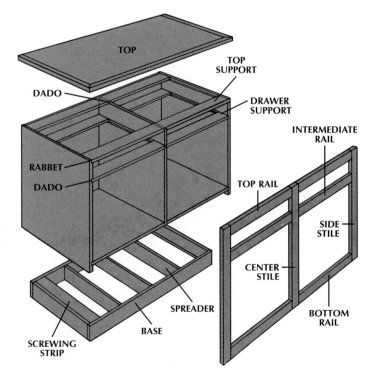

Sizing the parts.

A set of two-dimensional views, like the ones shown here for the cabinet on the opposite page, help you figure out the exact size of component parts. Include all parts, such as the drawer's construction front and false front *(page 72)*, in these drawings. The plans show how the dimensions of a structure's parts are deter-mined by clearances required for doors and drawers—and by allowances for wood thickness. To establish the sizes of the doors and drawer false fronts, draw lines representing the $1\frac{1}{2}$-inch width of the cabinet's face frame and then draw lines indicating the overlap for the drawers and doors, as shown on pages 60 and 61.

TOP

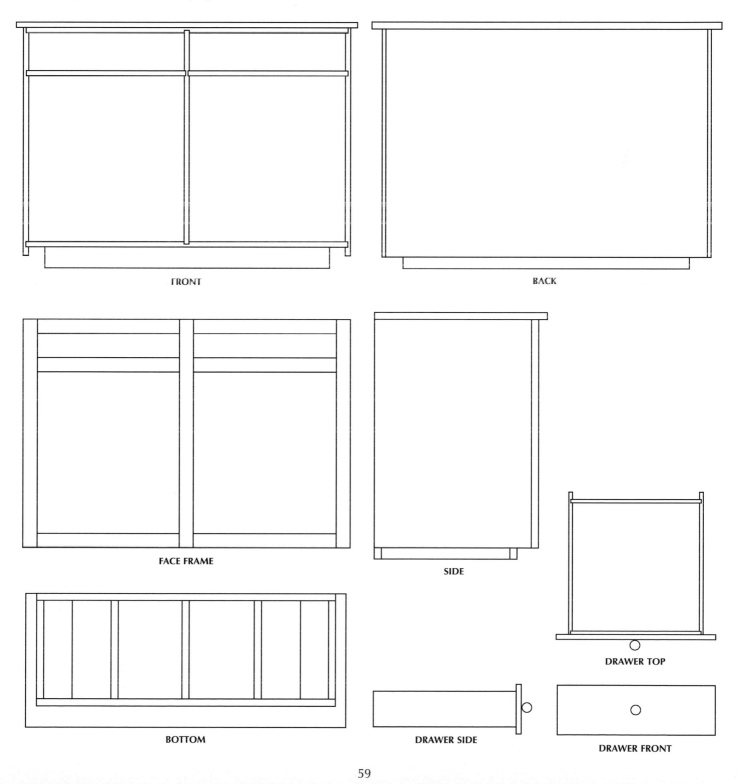

FRONT

BACK

FACE FRAME

SIDE

DRAWER TOP

BOTTOM

DRAWER SIDE

DRAWER FRONT

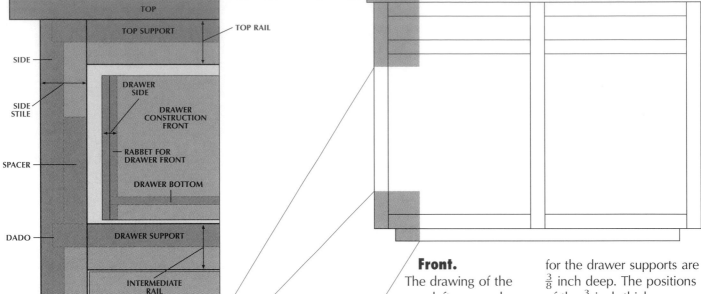

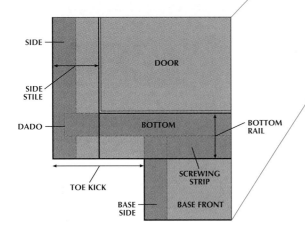

Front.

The drawing of the upper left corner shows the actual $\frac{1}{2}$-inch thickness and $4\frac{3}{4}$-inch height of the drawer side, as well as other details of drawer construction, such as the rabbet for the drawer front and the dado for the drawer bottom *(page 72)*. The section calls for a $\frac{1}{2}$-inch clearance for drawer glides between the drawer side and the spacer inside the cabinet *(page 75)*. Rabbets for the top supports and dadoes for the drawer supports are $\frac{3}{8}$ inch deep. The positions of the $\frac{3}{4}$-inch-thick carcass sides, top supports, and drawer supports are shown in relation to the $1\frac{1}{2}$-inch width of face frame components *(page 66)*.

At the base, a $\frac{3}{8}$-inch dado accommodates the cabinet's bottom. The drawing also shows the recessed base in relation to the cabinet's bottom and sides and the toe-kick space between the cabinet side and the base.

Top side.

This view clarifies details of the drawer and upper corner of the cabinet that are not visible in the front section *(above)*, including the top and bottom overlap of the drawer's false front and the distance the top overhangs the front of the cabinet.

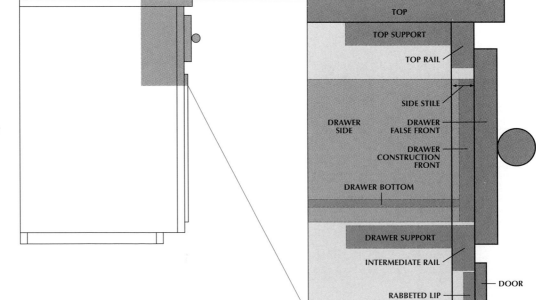

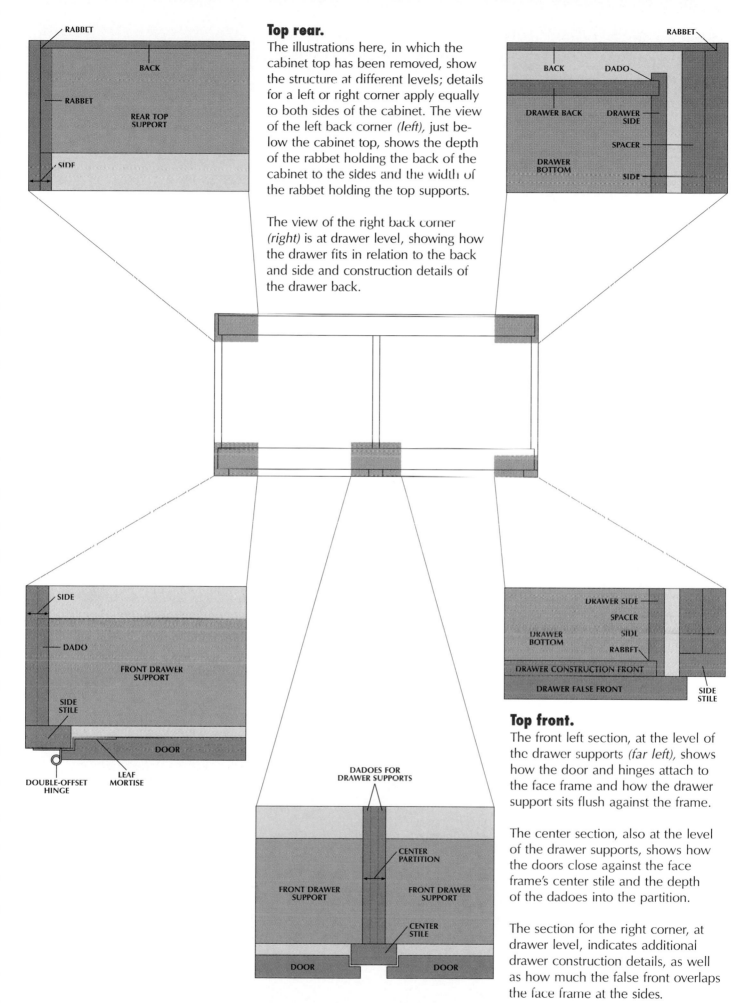

Top rear.

The illustrations here, in which the cabinet top has been removed, show the structure at different levels; details for a left or right corner apply equally to both sides of the cabinet. The view of the left back corner *(left),* just below the cabinet top, shows the depth of the rabbet holding the back of the cabinet to the sides and the width of the rabbet holding the top supports.

The view of the right back corner *(right)* is at drawer level, showing how the drawer fits in relation to the back and side and construction details of the drawer back.

RABBET

BACK

RABBET

REAR TOP SUPPORT

SIDE

RABBET

BACK   DADO

DRAWER BACK   DRAWER SIDE

SPACER

DRAWER BOTTOM

SIDE

SIDE

DADO

FRONT DRAWER SUPPORT

SIDE STILE

DOUBLE-OFFSET HINGE   LEAF MORTISE

DOOR

DRAWER SIDE

SPACER

DRAWER BOTTOM   SIDE

RABBET

DRAWER CONSTRUCTION FRONT

DRAWER FALSE FRONT

SIDE STILE

DADOES FOR DRAWER SUPPORTS

CENTER PARTITION

FRONT DRAWER SUPPORT   FRONT DRAWER SUPPORT

CENTER STILE

DOOR   DOOR

Top front.

The front left section, at the level of the drawer supports *(far left),* shows how the door and hinges attach to the face frame and how the drawer support sits flush against the frame.

The center section, also at the level of the drawer supports, shows how the doors close against the face frame's center stile and the depth of the dadoes into the partition.

The section for the right corner, at drawer level, indicates additional drawer construction details, as well as how much the false front overlaps the face frame at the sides.

61

Building the Cabinet Carcass

After you formulate a plan and buy materials for a cabinet *(pages 58-61)* you can begin the process of construction. If your cabinet is too big to be maneuvered in one piece from the workshop to its planned location, or if it is longer than 8 feet—the length of a sheet of plywood—build it in sections *(page 90)* and fit the mod-ules together as you install the unit.

An Organized Approach: Before assembling the cabinet, saw all parts of the carcass to size. Start by cutting the large components, such as the cabinet top, back, and sides, from plywood panels *(below)*.

Next, cut the smaller base com-ponents, top supports, and drawer supports from pieces of solid lum-ber or plywood that has been ripped to size. Finally, cut all rabbets and dadoes *(page 17)*.

Test-fit all joints before applying glue *(page 37)* and nailing the car-cass together *(pages 63-65)* or fas-tening it with screws.

 TOOLS

Table saw or
  circular saw
Electric drill
Screwdriver
Hammer
Nail set
Tape measure

 **MATERIALS**

Plywood ($\frac{3}{4}$" and
  $\frac{1}{4}$")
Parting bead
  (1 x 2)
Lumber (1 x 4 and
  1 x 6)
Glue
Finishing nails
  ($1\frac{1}{2}$" and 2")
Common nails
  ($1\frac{1}{8}$")
Flat-head screws
  ($1\frac{1}{4}$")

 **SAFETY TIPS**

Always wear eye protection when cutting with a power saw and when hammering nails.

ASSEMBLING THE BOX

RIP FENCE

1. Cutting the plywood.
To cut a strip of plywood to the necessary width *(pages 12-13)*, adjust a table saw's rip fence to the correct position. Place the panel with the good side up and have a helper hold it tight against the rip fence as you feed the plywood through the saw. Near the end of the cut, push the plywood with a push stick to keep your fingers clear of the blade.

If using a circular saw, position the panel good side down and clamp a straightedge cutting guide to it *(page 11)*. Make sure the plywood is well supported on both sides of the cut line.

2. Making the base.

◆ For the front and back, use $\frac{3}{4}$-inch boards or plywood cut to the width of the cabinet, if both ends will abut walls or other cabinets. If one end is exposed, cut front and back pieces 3 inches shorter for a toe-kick space; cut them 6 inches shorter if both ends are exposed.

◆ To create a 3-inch toe-kick space at the cabinet's front, cut spreaders and screwing strips *(page 58)* $4\frac{1}{2}$ inches shorter than its depth.
◆ Glue and nail the sides, front, and back together, then install the spreaders.
◆ At each end, nail a 4-inch-wide screwing strip flush with the top edges of the base.

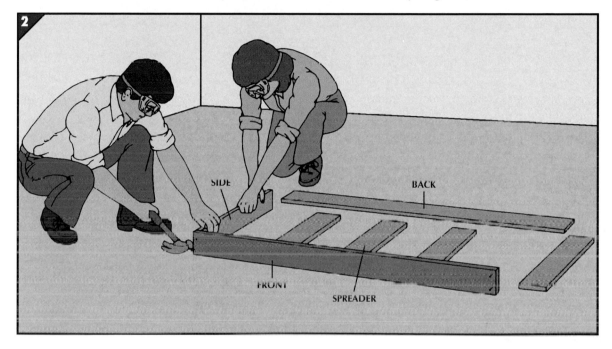

3. Fastening the carcass.

◆ Test-fit the side and bottom pieces, then mark lines on the outside faces of the boards to correspond to the middle of each dado.
◆ With the boards lying flat, start 2-inch finishing nails along the lines every 4 inches, beginning 1 inch from the edges.
◆ Squeeze a small bead of glue in the dado in one side and onto the end of the cabinet bottom and slide the two together, front edges on the floor. Drive the nails through the sides into the bottom, then glue and nail the other side.

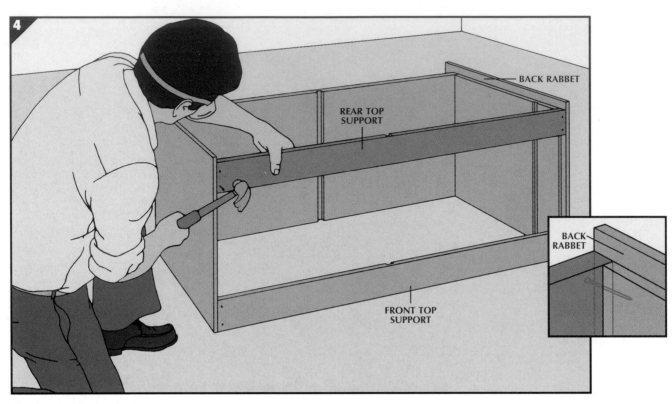

BACK RABBET

REAR TOP
SUPPORT

BACK
RABBET

FRONT TOP
SUPPORT

4. Installing top supports.
◆ Glue and nail the top supports to the rabbet at the top of each side, angling the nails slightly outward through the rabbet into the sides *(inset).* When attaching the rear top support, keep the back edge flush with the inside edge of the back rabbet.

◆ Apply glue to the partition's ends and to the dadoes in the top supports and bottom. Then slide the partition into the dadoes and drive 2-inch finishing nails through the bottom and top supports and into the partition.

5. Squaring the cabinet.
◆ Working with a helper, hook the end of a tape measure on one corner of the cabinet and measure diagonally to the opposite corner; measure the other diagonal in the same way.

◆ If the measurements differ, push the corners of the longer one toward each other and let them spring back, then remeasure both diagonals. Repeat the adjustment until the measurements are equal, then set all the nails.

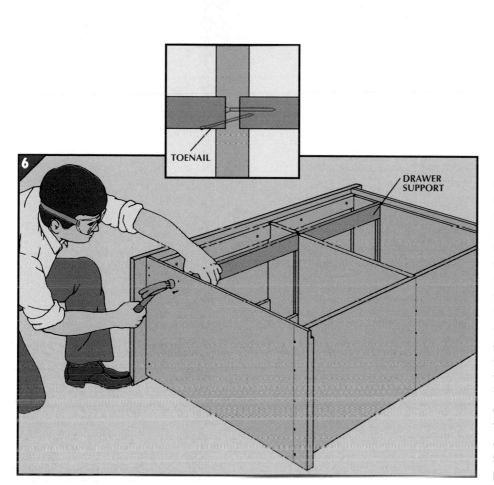

TOENAIL

DRAWER
SUPPORT

6. Installing the supports.
◆ Apply glue to the top supports and place the top on the supports so that it is centered on the cabinet and flush with the back.
◆ Drill pilot holes up through the top supports into the top, then secure the top to the cabinet with $1\frac{1}{4}$-inch flat-head screws.
◆ Nail drawer supports between the dadoes in the sides and partition.
◆ Glue and nail the supports in place with 2-inch finishing nails, positioning the front supports flush with the front of the cabinet and the rear ones flush with the inside of the back rabbet. At a partition (inset), nail straight into the supports on one side; toenail the supports on the other side.

7. Attaching the back and base.
◆ Cut the cabinet back from the corner of a sheet of $\frac{1}{4}$-inch plywood.
◆ Apply glue to the side rabbets and to the edges of the top support, the bottom, the drawer supports, and the partition.
◆ Drive $1\frac{1}{8}$-inch nails through the back into the side rabbets, top supports, bottom, drawer supports, and partition at 3-inch intervals (right). Angle the nails slightly outward into the rabbets (Step 4, inset).
◆ Place the cabinet on its back and center the assembled base against the bottom.
◆ Drive four $1\frac{1}{4}$-inch flat-head screws through each screwing strip (page 63, Step 2) in the base and into the bottom of the cabinet.

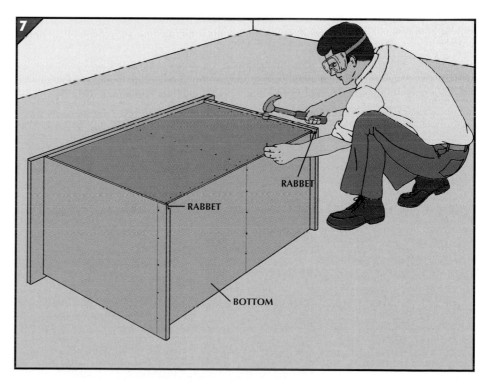

RABBET

RABBET

BOTTOM

Framing the Cabinet Front

The face frame covering the unfinished plywood edges at the front of a cabinet is built of 1-by-2 lumber—pine or poplar for cabinets to be painted, birch for stained cabinets, and occasionally fine hardwoods such as cherry and oak. As shown opposite, there are two ways to assemble such a structure. One style of face frame has pieces that are simpler to cut than those of the other but result in a frame with more joints to assemble.

Cut the frame's pieces with special precision; tiny errors multiply with successive cuts. To cut pieces of identical length on a table saw, it's best to use a stop block on a miter gauge extension *(page 73)* rather than cut lines drawn on the lumber. When using a circular saw, clamp same-sized pieces together and cut them with a single pass.

Joining the Parts: There are a couple of ways to fasten either style of face frame together. The simpler is to assemble the components with biscuits—thin pieces of compressed wood. They are glued into slots cut in the edges and ends of the boards with a plate joiner *(opposite),* which is available from tool-rental centers.

Alternatively, you can substitute dowels for biscuits. Use grooved, or fluted, dowels. The grooves allow glue to escape from the hole as the dowel is inserted. Fluted dowels are available at most hardware stores or home centers, precut to the correct length.

Making a face frame that is fastened with dowels is more demanding than assembling it with biscuits. Unlike biscuit slots, which tolerate positioning errors of $\frac{1}{16}$ inch, the holes for dowels must be marked perfectly and drilled squarely with the help of a doweling jig, dowel centers, and a brad-point drill bit *(page 71)*.

TOOLS

Table saw or circular saw
Plate joiner
Combination squar
Bar clamps
Block plane
Sanding block
Electric drill and bits
Hammer
Doweling jig
Dowel centers

MATERIALS

1 x 2s
Compressed-beech
  biscuits
Glue *(page 37)*
Fluted dowels
Sandpaper
Finishing nails (2")

SAFETY TIPS

Protect your eyes with safety goggles when you are hammering nails, cutting with a power saw, or operating a plate joiner.

Face-Frame Rules

When laying out a face frame, keep in mind the following relationships between the frame and the cabinet:

✔ Align the top of the top rail flush with the top edge of the top support.

✔ Position the top of the bottom rail so it is flush with the carcass floor.

✔ Place the outsides of the side stiles flush with the carcass sides.

✔ In a cabinet with multiple stacks of drawers, position the center stile on the middle partition between the drawers.

✔ Set intermediate rails flush with the tops of drawer supports.

TWO WAYS TO BUILD A FACE FRAME

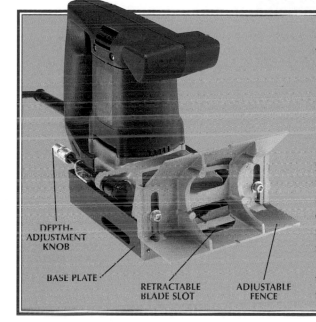

TOP RAIL
INTERMEDIATE RAIL
CENTER STILE
SIDE STILE
SLOT
BOTTOM RAIL
BISCUIT

An easy-to-cut frame.
Only two lengths of wood are used in a face frame constructed as shown at left—and in the procedure for building a face frame that begins on page 68. All stiles are one length, all rails another. In this case, the pieces are joined by wooden biscuits *(photograph)* that absorb moisture from the glue, swelling within the slots of mating pieces to form a tight joint.

When using biscuits, dry-fit all pieces with a biscuit in each slot before applying glue. Because the biscuits absorb moisture quickly, a biscuit joint with glue is virtually impossible to separate or adjust within a minute or so of joining. Always store biscuits in a dry place in a sealed plastic bag.

BISCUITS

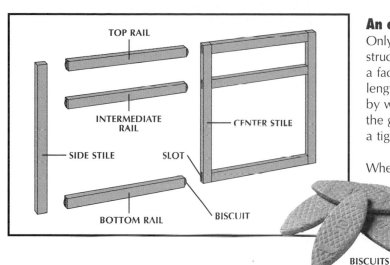

DEPTH-ADJUSTMENT KNOB
BASE PLATE
RETRACTABLE BLADE SLOT
ADJUSTABLE FENCE

CUTTING SLOTS MADE EASIER

This ingenious tool, called a plate joiner or a biscuit joiner, has made cabinet joinery much easier while providing solid, strong joints.

As the face of the plate joiner is pressed against the edge of a board, a retractable blade in the tool cuts a semicircular slot in the edge of the board. A movable fence on the front of the tool rests on the face of the board and slides up and down to center the cutting slot on the edge of the board. The blade can be adjusted to cut slots of different depths for the three standard sizes of biscuits: When you are working with 1-by-2 boards for a face frame, adjust the knob to 0 to cut slots for No. 0 biscuits, the smallest that are available.

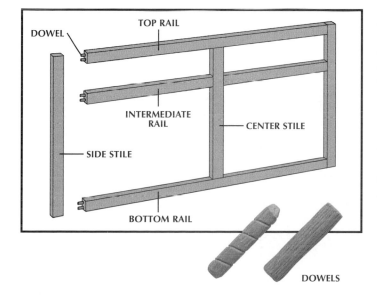

DOWEL
TOP RAIL
INTERMEDIATE RAIL
CENTER STILE
SIDE STILE
BOTTOM RAIL
DOWELS

A frame that minimizes joints.
This design requires two fewer joints than the frame above, but rails are cut to two different lengths, as are stiles. The top and bottom rails are single long pieces, whereas the intermediate rail consists of two shorter components. Side stiles are longer than the center stile. Each joint of the frame illustrated here is fastened with a pair of fluted dowels, which come in two interchangeable varieties *(photographs)*.

ASSEMBLING A FRAME WITH WOOD BISCUITS

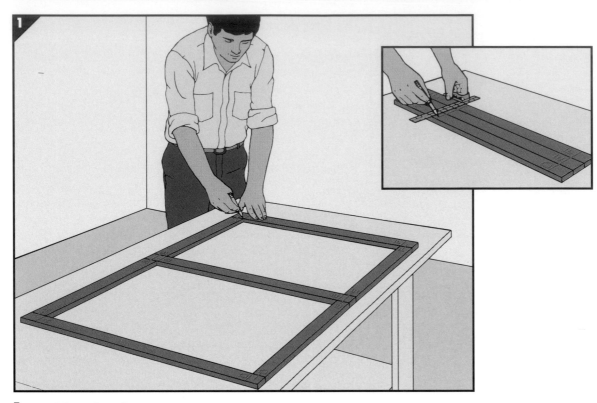

1. Marking the pieces.

◆ After cutting the stiles and rails, lay out the stiles and the top and bottom rails faceup on a workbench. Letter the joints for identification.

◆ Make sure the pieces are aligned correctly, then draw lines on the edge and face of each stile to mark the corners of the joint *(above)*. Also mark a guideline for the plate joiner across the center of each rail-stile joint.

◆ For intermediate rails, measure from the top of the carcass to the top of each drawer support, mark the measured distance down from the top of a stile, and mark the stile for the top of each intermediate rail.

◆ Set each stile alongside the marked stile; transfer the marks across them with a combination square *(inset)*.

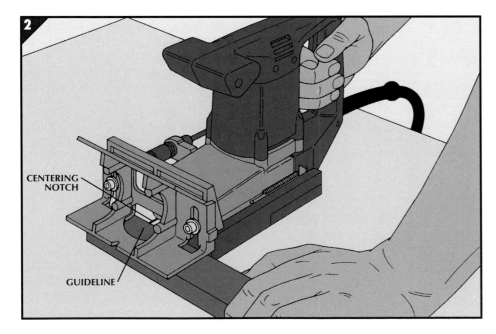

2. Cutting the slots.

◆ Position the plate joiner on one of the face frame pieces as shown at left and adjust the front fence to center the blade on the edge of the board. Set the depth of cut for No. 0 biscuits.

◆ Align the centering notch of the joiner with the guideline on the board.

◆ Switch on the tool and push it into the edge of the board to cut the slot.

◆ Repeat the procedure for all the slots remaining to be cut.

CENTERING NOTCH

GUIDELINE

3. Joining rails and stiles.

◆ After cutting all slots, test-fit the frame with No. 0 biscuits in the slots but without glue. Reslot any joints that don't align.

◆ Beginning at the top left of the frame where the left stile joins the top rail and working one joint at a time, squeeze glue into each slot of mating pieces and along the edges where they meet. Make sure the glue evenly coats the inside surfaces of each slot.

◆ Assemble the joint quickly before the biscuit begins to expand.

◆ Repeat for the remaining joints, working from top to bottom, left to right on the frame.

BISCUIT

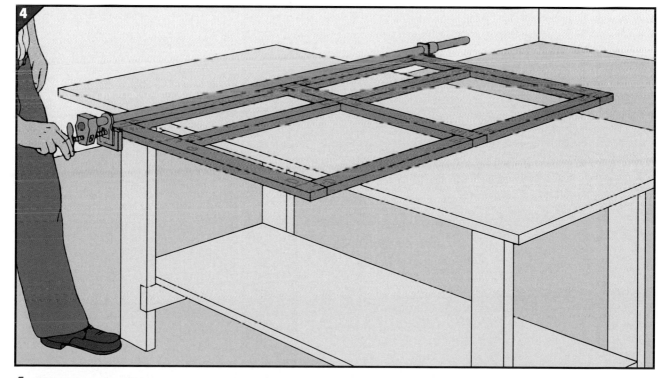

4. Clamping the frame.

◆ Set the frame across a workbench, overhanging each side, and fasten bar clamps across the frame at the top and bottom rails, protecting the stiles with scraps of wood. Tighten the clamps until glue is forced from the joints.

◆ Measure the diagonals to ensure the frame is square (page 64, Step 5); if it is not, reset the clamps at a slight angle across the frame to pull it into square.

◆ Sight across the frame's top to determine if there are twists; if necessary, pull the low corner sharply upward to flatten the frame.

◆ When the frame is square and flat, loosen each clamp about a quarter-turn.

◆ Turn the clamped frame over, rest the clamps on the workbench, and fasten a clamp across each intermediate rail.

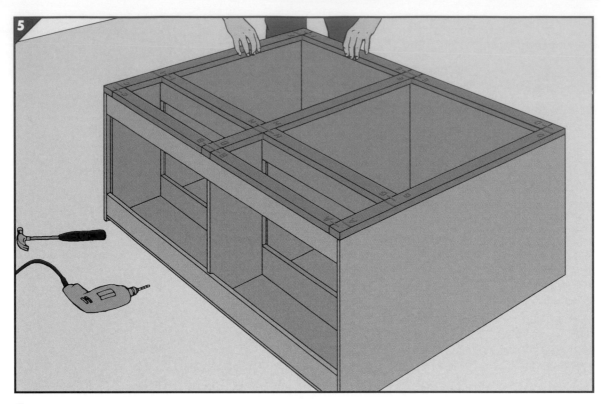

5. Attaching the face frame.

◆ Set the frame on the carcass of the cabinet and then check the fit. For a frame that is slightly large, plan to plane or sand the edges flush after nailing it to the carcass. Align a frame that is too small with the bottom and one side of the carcass.

◆ Glue the frame to the carcass edges. Every 6 inches, drill a pilot hole through the frame into the carcass edge.

◆ Drive a 2-inch finishing nail into each hole.

Start at a corner and nail the sides first. Check frame alignment before you drive each nail; if the plywood is bowed, force it straight with your hand or with bar clamps.

◆ After fastening the sides, nail the center stile and the rails, then set all the nails.

⚠️ **CAUTION** *When you are planing or sanding overhanging frame edges, take care to avoid marring the carcass.*

JOINTS MADE WITH DOWELS

1. Marking the stiles.

◆ Mark the corners where rails and stiles meet *(page 68)*, but omit the centering marks across the joints. Then set the stiles side by side, with marked edges upward.

◆ Clamp the stiles together and mark for the hole centers that join the top and bottom rails to the stiles. Draw lines across all of the edges simultaneously with a combination square, $\frac{1}{2}$ inch and 1 inch from each end of the stiles; mark for intermediate rails $\frac{1}{2}$ inch and 1 inch from each rail edge previously marked on the stiles.

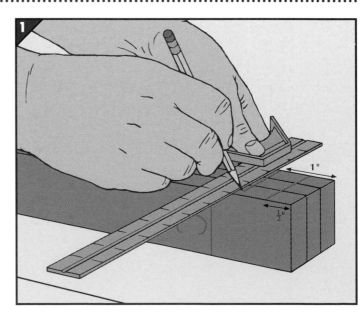

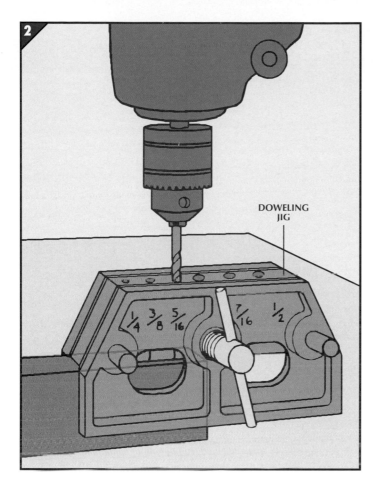

2. Drilling the stiles.

To ensure perpendicular holes of uniform depth, use a doweling jig with a depth stop set to $1\frac{1}{8}$ inch.

◆ Tighten the jig on the edge of a stile. Align tick marks engraved within the jig's $\frac{5}{16}$-inch opening directly alongside a dowel mark.

◆ Because the opening in the jig is slightly larger than $\frac{5}{16}$ inch to permit the drill bit to spin freely, drill with a $\frac{5}{16}$-inch brad-point bit, whose sharp point prevents the bit from "walking" off-center before the metal bites into the wood.

◆ Repeat the procedure for each dowel hole marking on the stiles.

BRAD-POINT BIT

3. Drilling the rails.

Dowel centers allow precise alignment of dowel holes in the rails with those in the stiles.

◆ Insert a $\frac{5}{16}$-inch dowel center in each dowel hole at one end of a stile.

◆ Align the adjoining rail with the stile, and push the rail against the points of the dowel centers to leave small indentations in the end of the rail.

◆ Use the doweling jig and brad-point bit as described above to drill dowel holes in the rail.

◆ Repeat the process for the remaining rail ends.

◆ Squeeze a small amount of glue into each dowel hole of a joint and on the edges of pieces where they touch. Press a dowel into place, then assemble the joint.

◆ Complete the frame in the same order described in Step 3 on page 69.

DOWEL CENTER

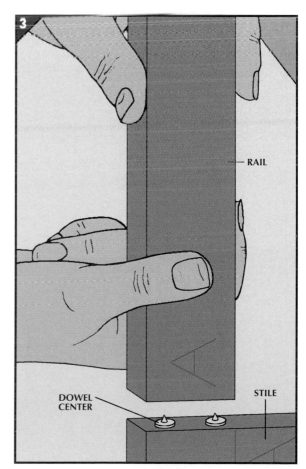

RAIL

DOWEL
CENTER

STILE

Adding drawers is the first step in transforming an open carcass into a finished cabinet. Because drawers are moved frequently, they are subject to a lot of stress and so must be constructed with strong joints and from sturdy stock.

The Basic Drawer: A drawer is essentially a box without a lid. The front of a drawer is usually made of two pieces. One, called a construction front, forms a side of the box; the other, called a false front, is attached to the construction front *(below)*. This combination lets you conceal the less-expensive wood used for the box behind a facade of more-attractive wood.

Drawer Fronts: The simplest drawer to make and the most commonly employed is the lipped drawer, on which the front overlaps the cabinet frame. Because the overlap conceals any irregularities of fit between the drawer and its opening, this design requires no finicky sanding and planing.

Less common because of the difficulty of achieving an exact fit is the flush drawer, whose front fits flush with the drawer opening so that the face of the cabinet is uninterrupted by projections. For this style you must cut the false front precisely to create equal clearances of $\frac{1}{16}$ inch all around. Do not make a false front for a flush drawer until the drawer has been assembled and mounted on its glides *(page 77)*.

Making a Drawer: The back, sides, and construction front of a drawer are generally cut from plywood or lumber at least $\frac{1}{2}$ inch thick; bottoms are plywood at least $\frac{1}{4}$ inch thick; and false fronts are plywood or lumber $\frac{3}{4}$ inch thick.

A strong drawer uses a pattern of rabbets and dadoes that can be cut with a router *(page 15)*, a table saw *(page 12-13)*, or even a handsaw and chisel. For an extra-strong drawer, attach the front with a double-dado joint *(opposite)*.

In the course of construction, test-fit drawer pieces and check them for squareness before you glue, clamp, and nail the joints.

Glides and Runners: The mechanism that guides a drawer's movement is critical to the overall dimensions of the drawer. Traditionally the drawers in fine furniture slide on wood runners *(page 76)*, but in modern cabinets commercial metal glides are generally preferred for their sturdiness, ease of installation, and smooth operation.

With glides, the drawer is made narrower than the opening to provide space for the glides—generally $\frac{1}{2}$ inch on each side.

 TOOLS

Table saw or circular saw
Router
C clamps
Tenoning jig

Electric drill
Screwdriver
Hand-screw clamps

SAFETY TIPS *Protect your eyes with goggles or safety glasses when hammering, when cutting with a power saw, or when operating a router.*

THE BASIC DRAWER

A false-front drawer.
The bottom of this drawer slips into $\frac{1}{4}$- by $\frac{1}{4}$-inch dadoes located $\frac{1}{2}$ inch from the lower edge of each side and the back. The back fits into $\frac{3}{4}$-inch vertical dadoes cut $\frac{1}{4}$ inch deep and $\frac{1}{2}$ inch from the back edge of both sides. Quarter-inch rabbets at the other end of both sides accept the drawer's construction front, to which the false front is fastened with screws and glue. All joints but those involving the bottom are held with glue and $1\frac{1}{2}$-inch finishing nails.

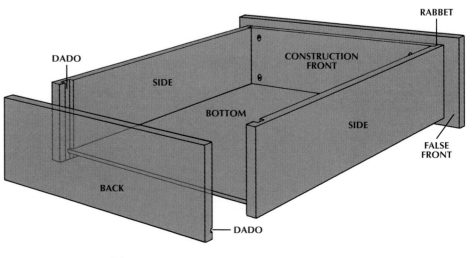

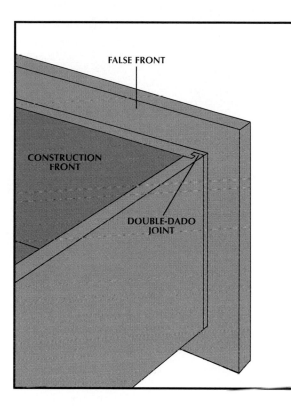

An extra-strength front.

To assure that the front of a drawer will stand up to hard use, attach the construction front to the sides with double-dado joints, as shown at left, instead of rabbets.

CUTTING A DOUBLE-DADO JOINT

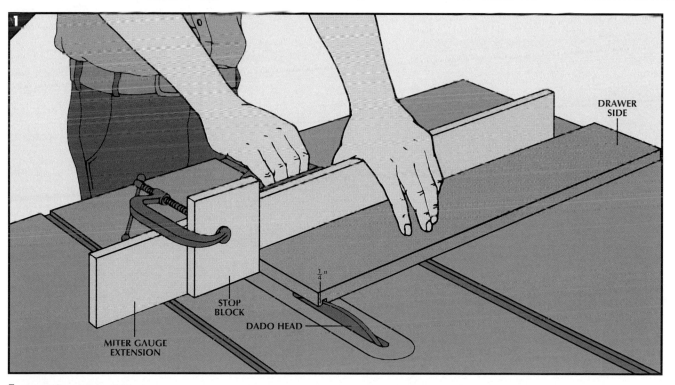

1. Dadoing the sides.

◆ On a table saw, shown here without a blade guard for clarity, mount a $\frac{1}{4}$-inch dado head (page 18) and set it to a height of $\frac{5}{16}$ inch.

◆ Clamp a stop block to a miter gauge extension so that when you butt the front end of a drawer side against the block, the dado head will cut $\frac{1}{4}$ inch from the board's end.

◆ Hold the drawer side against the miter gauge and stop block, and cut the dado.

◆ Cut a dado in the other side of the drawer in the same manner.

To cut the dadoes with a router, fit it with a $\frac{1}{4}$-inch dado bit and set the bit $\frac{5}{16}$ inch deep. Use a board to guide the bit $\frac{1}{4}$ inch from the front end of the side (page 17).

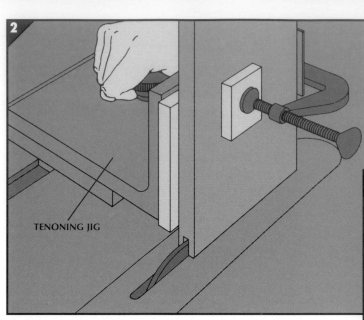

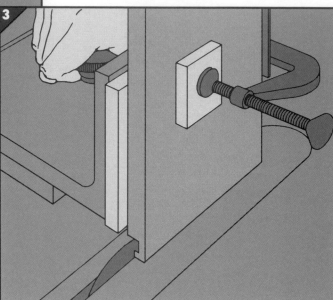

2. Dadoing the front.

◆ Mount a tenoning jig in the right-hand miter slot of a table saw, and clamp the drawer front, protected by wood blocks, against it. Position the work piece with its inside face toward the jig and its front edge on the table.

◆ Set the height of the dado head to $\frac{1}{4}$ inch, adjust the jig to center the work piece on the dado head, and push the jig along the miter slot to cut the dado.

◆ Reposition the drawer front to cut the dado in the opposite end.

If you are dadoing with a router instead of a table saw, use a slotting bit that cuts a groove $\frac{1}{4}$ inch wide and $\frac{1}{4}$ inch deep.

⚠ **CAUTION** *The table-saw blade guard must be removed to make this cut and the one in the next step. Work with extreme caution around the exposed blade.*

3. Completing drawer-side tenons.

◆ With the tenoning jig still on the table, replace the dado head with a regular saw blade.

◆ Clamp a drawer side to the jig with the dado facing the jig as shown above.

◆ Set the saw blade to a height of $\frac{5}{16}$ inch, and position the jig so that the blade cuts $\frac{1}{4}$ inch off the front edge of the dado.

◆ Perform the same operation on the other drawer side.

If you are using a router, set the depth at $\frac{5}{16}$ inch and guide the tool with a clamped board.

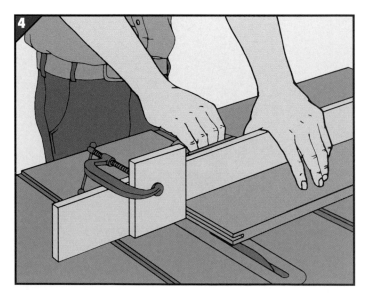

4. Trimming the tenons.

◆ Leave the saw blade at a height of $\frac{5}{16}$ inch, and snug the drawer front—with its inside facedown—against a miter gauge extension and a stop block positioned so that the blades will cut $\frac{1}{4}$ inch off the end of the board as shown at left *(blade guard removed for clarity)*.

◆ Push the board through the saw, then reposition and trim the other end.

If you are using a router, set the depth at $\frac{5}{16}$ inch and guide the tool with a clamped board.

INSTALLING DRAWER GLIDES

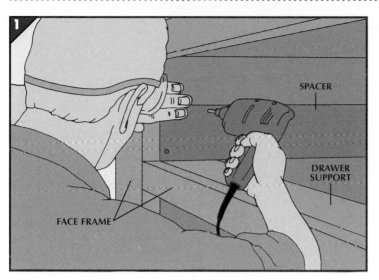

1. Attaching spacers.

◆ From $\frac{3}{4}$-inch plywood, cut a spacer as long as the cabinet is deep and at least 3 inches wide. Make two spacers for each drawer.

◆ Set each spacer, edge up, on a drawer support and against the cabinet side or center partition.

◆ With a combination bit *(page 14)*, bore pilot holes for $1\frac{1}{4}$-inch flat-head screws, then drive them through the spacer and into the side or partition.

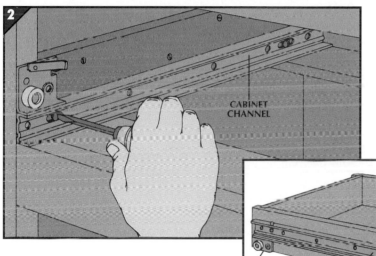

2. Mounting the glides.

◆ Set a cabinet channel on the carcass drawer supports and flush with the front of the cabinet, then mark the centers of the channel's oblong holes. Postpone marking the round holes until Step 3.

◆ Drill pilot holes at the marks, then fasten the channel to the spacer with the screws that are provided by the manufacturer.

◆ Fasten the other cabinet channel on the opposite side of the drawer opening.

◆ Drill pilot holes and screw the drawer channels to the sides of the drawer through the oblong holes. Typically, the channel is mounted with the roller flange toward the back of the drawer and positioned on the side of the drawer as shown in the inset.

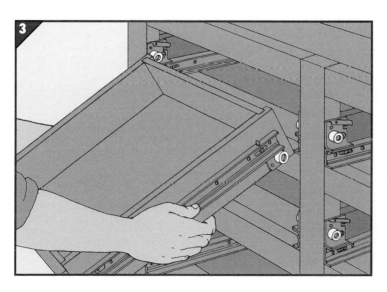

3. Adjusting the glides.

◆ Slide the drawer channels into the cabinet channels.

◆ Check the drawer's position; it should close against the cabinet's front, with equal clearances all around.

◆ To adjust the drawer, loosen the drawer-channel screws and move the channel up or down, or loosen the cabinet-channel screws and slide the channel forward or backward.

◆ When the drawer fits, drill pilot holes and drive screws through the circular screw holes in both channels. Tighten all the screws.

A DRAWER WITH WOOD RUNNERS

1. Marking and installing the runners.
On some cabinets, metal drawer glides would clash with the style of the piece. In such a case, mount wood runners inside the drawer opening and cut grooves in the sides of the drawer as glides, as shown on this page, before installing the false front.

◆ Mount wood spacers along the cabinet sides *(page 75)*.

◆ Cut two runners from $\frac{3}{4}$-inch square molding, each as long as the cabinet is deep.

◆ Inside the cabinet, place a combination square against the top and mark a point half the height of the drawer, plus $\frac{3}{8}$ inch (half the thickness of the runner), plus $\frac{1}{8}$ inch for clearance.

◆ Screw the runners to the wood spacers, countersinking the screwheads.

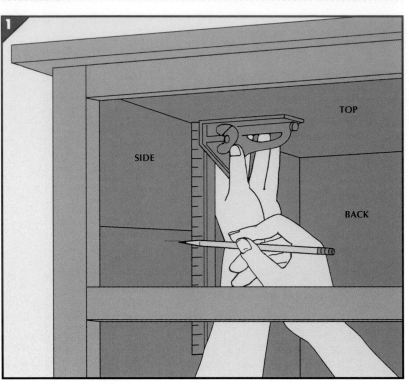

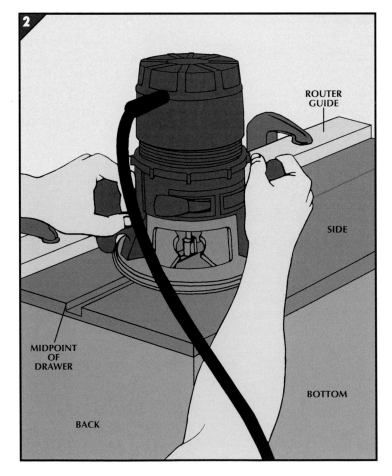

2. Cutting runner guides.
◆ Draw a line marking each drawer side's midpoint.

◆ With a $\frac{3}{4}$-inch bit, cut a $\frac{1}{4}$-inch-deep dado below the line, using a straight board as a guide *(left)*. Sand the grooves with 120-grit sandpaper.

◆ Slide the drawer onto the runners. If the fit is too tight, sand the groove with 100-grit sandpaper until the drawer moves smoothly.

◆ When the fit is correct, coat both the runners and the grooves with paste wax.

1. Marking for a good fit.

A false front that overlaps a face frame is made in much the same way as the false front shown on this page, which fits within the drawer opening. Constructing the flush-drawer variety, however, requires greater precision.

◆ Measure a drawer opening, then from $\frac{3}{4}$ inch-thick wood cut a false front $\frac{1}{8}$ inch narrower and $\frac{1}{8}$ inch shorter. Deal with multiple openings separately; their dimensions may vary.

◆ Open the drawer partway. Holding the false front against the construction front and overlapping it evenly on all sides, mark guidelines on the back of the false front along the top and sides of the construction front *(right)*.

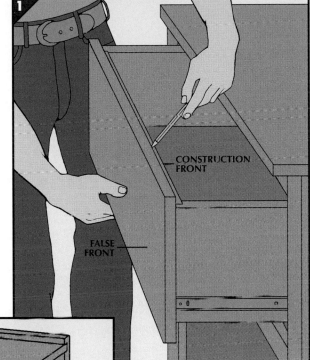

2. Attaching the front.

◆ Place the false front facedown on a workbench.

◆ Set the drawer on the false front, aligned with the guidelines. Mark another line on the back of the false front indicating the bottom edge of the drawer. Remove the drawer and cut the false front along this line.

◆ Spread glue within the guidelines on the back of the false front, then clamp the drawer and the false front together and to the workbench.

◆ Working from the inside *(left)*, drill two pilot holes—the exact position is not critical—through the construction front and halfway into the false front. Secure the false front to the construction front with $1\frac{1}{4}$-inch flathead screws.

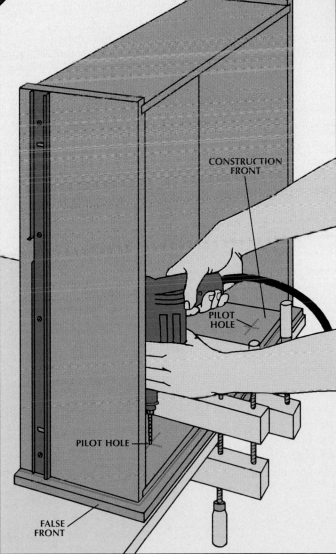

A final touch in turning open shelves into cabinets is the addition of doors. The usual way to mount a door is to place the hinges so that the door swings to one side, but it can also open upward or downward. A door that is hinged at the bottom can double as a work surface if it pivots on a sturdy kind of hinge called a piano hinge and is braced by stay supports *(page 85)*.

Door Styles: A door with a lipped or overlapping fit against the cabinet front is easier to build than a door set within an opening because it forgives slight errors in measurement and construction.

The door style you choose should reflect the cabinet's character and the tools at your disposal. The options range from a plain panel door cut from high-quality plywood to a relatively sophisticated frame-and-panel design *(page 80)*.

A frame-and-panel door calls for precise measuring and cutting if the pieces are to fit together neatly. A table saw simplifies the construction of any door, and is especially useful when building the raised-panel variety. Nonetheless, you can handle the job of beveling the panel with a variable-speed router that is equipped with a special bit *(page 83)*.

Whatever door design you decide to build, choose hinges and latches *(pages 84-87)* that are appropriate for that style, both functionally and aesthetically.

Hinge Essentials: Hinges vary greatly in style and type, but the basic installation techniques that are shown on pages 87 to 89 apply to most of them.

The number and size of hinges required by a door depend on its dimensions. Two rules of thumb apply: First, on any door that is longer than 2 feet, install three hinges; second, the total length of the hinges should equal at least one-sixth the length of the hinged edge.

For example, if the door is 24 inches tall, use two 2-inch hinges; if the door is 72 inches tall, use three 4-inch hinges. When only two hinges are required, they are usually placed a quarter of the way from the top and bottom of the door; when three hinges are installed, one hinge is centered and the other two are placed 4 or 5 inches from the top and bottom.

TOOLS

Table saw or circular saw	Self-centering bit
Router	Chisel
C clamps	Mallet
Electric drill	Screwdriver
	Awl

SAFETY TIPS

Protect your eyes with goggles when using a hammer and chisel, a power saw, or a router.

DIFFERENT WAYS TO FIT DOORS

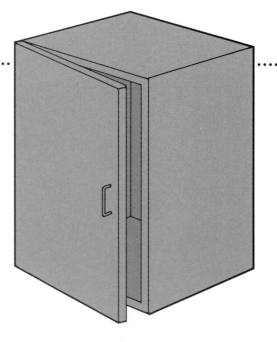

Overlapping door.
This type fits over the entire cabinet front, rather than into the opening, and is cut to fit flush with the sides, top, and bottom of the carcass. The door covers slight irregularities in the cabinet itself.

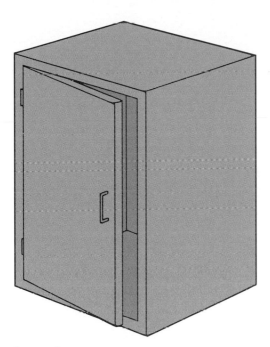

Inset door.

Because it fits inside the opening of the cabinet, the inset door must be cut and hinged carefully in order for it to open and close smoothly.

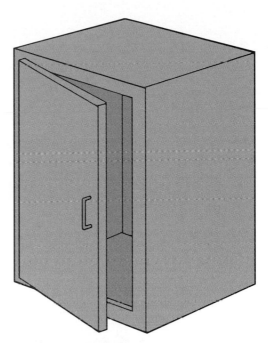

Partially overlapping.

A variation used for some cabinets with face frames (page 66), this door requires special hinges such as the semiconcealed variety shown on page 85.

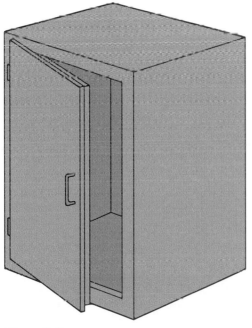

Lipped door.

This type fits both into and over the cabinet opening. The overlapping lip is usually made by cutting a rabbet around the edges, but the door can also be made by gluing two panels together. Because it requires hinges shaped to accommodate the lip, buy the hinges first, then cut the door to fit them.

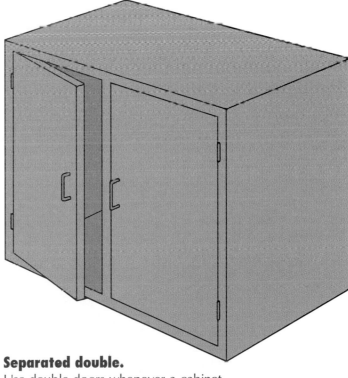

Separated double.

Use double doors whenever a cabinet opening is wider than it is high. This type is divided by a center stile, which gives the cabinet greater rigidity. The doors can be overlapping, lipped, or inset (shown here).

TWO STYLES OF DOORS

A plain panel door.
For a simple cabinet front, cut a door from plywood at least $\frac{1}{2}$ inch thick to the dimensions required for the door-hanging method that you choose *(pages 78-79)*. To make a lipped design *(right)*, cut the panel $\frac{1}{2}$ inch larger than the dimensions of the opening, then cut rabbets on the door's back edges to the size of the offset leaf of the hinges *(page 84)*—generally $\frac{3}{8}$ inch by $\frac{3}{8}$ inch.

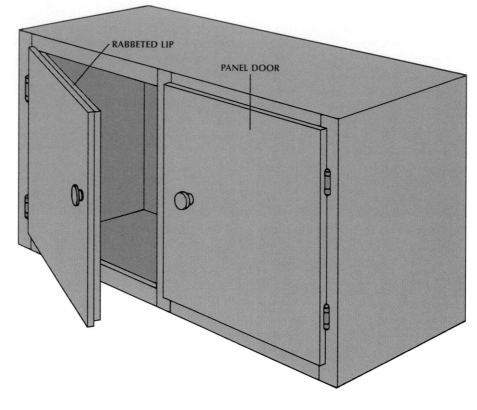

A frame-and-panel door.
In this elaborate structure, a frame of two vertical pieces called stiles and two horizontal pieces called rails—cut from 1-inch boards and glued together with mortise-and-tenon joints—encloses a decorative wood panel. In this example, called a raised-panel door, a panel cut from a board $\frac{3}{4}$ inch thick is beveled around the perimeter *(pages 82-83)* to create a raised center section. The panel fits into dadoes cut into the stiles and rails.

For a simpler design, fit a plain piece of $\frac{1}{4}$-inch plywood into the frame and cover the joint between frame and panel with quarter-round molding *(inset)*.

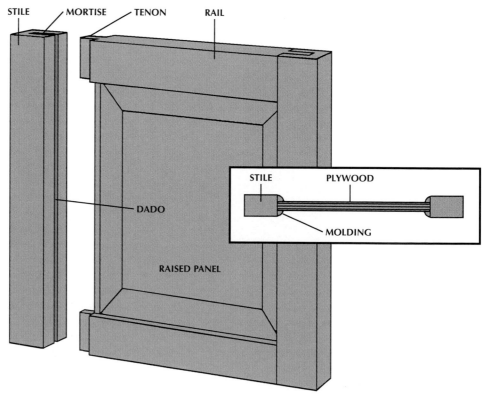

THE FRAME FOR A FRAME-AND-PANEL DOOR

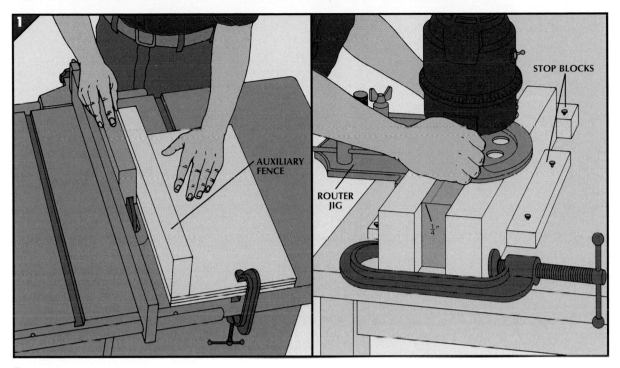

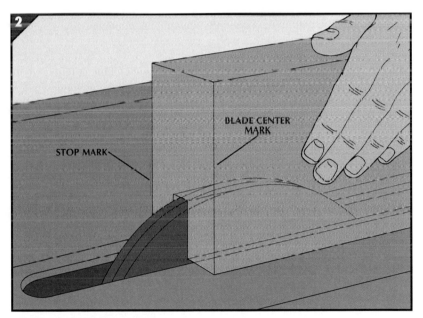

1. Dadoing the frame pieces.

◆ Cut stiles and rails from lumber that is $\frac{3}{4}$ inch thick.

◆ To cut grooves for the panel on a table saw *(above, left)*, remove the blade guard and fit the saw with a $\frac{1}{4}$-inch dado head *(page 10)*.

◆ Set the rip fence $\frac{1}{2}$ inch from the blade, then clamp an auxiliary fence—a 2-by-4 nailed to a piece of plywood— $\frac{3}{4}$ inch from the rip fence.

◆ Raise the dado head to a height of $\frac{1}{4}$ inch, then place a frame piece with its inside edge down and feed it across the blade.

◆ Dado the other pieces the same way.

◆ To cut these dadoes with a router *(above, right)*, clamp a frame piece, inside edge up, between scrap pieces and nail stop blocks to the worktable at the sides and at one end of the assembly to steady the work.

◆ Fit the router with a $\frac{1}{4}$-inch dadoing bit set to a cutting depth of $\frac{1}{4}$ inch, and use a router jig to guide the bit $\frac{1}{4}$ inch in from the edge of the frame piece as you cut the dado.

 The table-saw cuts here and in Step 2 cannot be made **CAUTION** *with the blade guard in place. Work with caution around the exposed blade.*

2. Mortising the stiles.

◆ To cut the mortises on a table saw, raise the dado head to a height of $1\frac{1}{16}$ inches and detach the auxiliary fence so you can more easily see guide marks necessary for this cut.

◆ Mark the fence at the center of the blade, then measure along the fence a distance equal to the rail width minus $\frac{1}{4}$ inch and make a stop mark.

◆ Position a stile as in Step 1, turn on the saw, and push the piece to the fence's stop mark.

◆ Turn the stile around to cut a mortise in the other end, then cut mortises in the other stile's ends.

◆ To form the mortises with a router, deepen the dadoes at the stile ends: Mark the stile edges a distance from the ends as long as the rail width less $\frac{1}{4}$ inch. Cut the mortises with repeated passes. Extend the bit in increments of no more than $\frac{3}{8}$ inch until you have deepened the cuts to $1\frac{1}{16}$ inches.

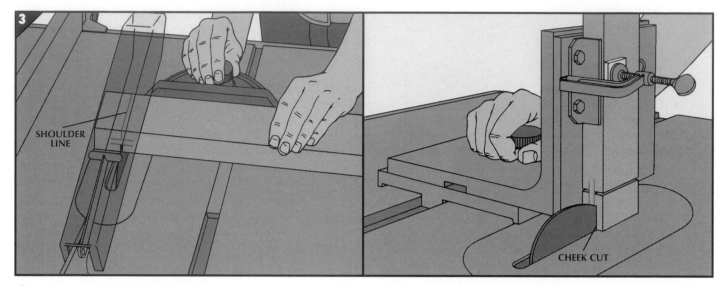

SHOULDER LINE

CHEEK CUT

3. Cutting tenons on the rails.

◆ Fit a table saw with an ordinary blade set to a cutting depth of $\frac{1}{4}$ inch.
◆ Mark lines—called shoulder lines—1 inch from each end of the rails. Use the miter gauge to cut across both faces of a rail along marked lines.
◆ To complete the tenons, secure the rail vertically in a tenoning jig *(page 74, Step 2)*, adjust the jig for a cut $\frac{1}{4}$ inch in from the outer face of the rail, set the blade height to 1 inch, and run the rail end across the blade for

a "cheek" cut. Turn the rail around to cut a second cheek.
◆ When all the frame pieces are shaped, test-assemble them and sand or chisel them as necessary for a perfect fit.

To make tenons with a router, cut rabbets that are $\frac{1}{4}$ inch deep and 1 inch wide.

⚠ **CAUTION** *The cut with the tenoning jig and in Step 2 (opposite) cannot be made with the guard in place. Work with caution around the exposed blade.*

SHAPING THE PANEL

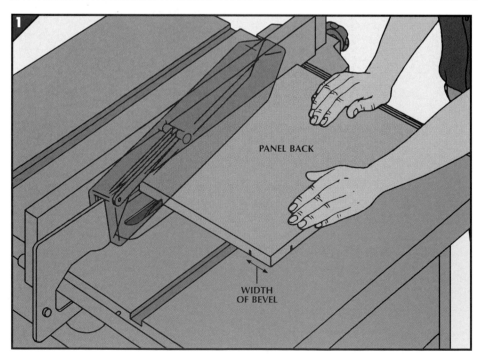

PANEL BACK

WIDTH OF BEVEL

1. Starting the bevel.

◆ From $\frac{3}{4}$-inch-thick stock, cut a panel $\frac{1}{4}$ inch smaller than the distance between the bottoms of the dadoes on opposite sides of the frame.
◆ Set the blade of a table saw to a cutting depth of $\frac{1}{16}$ inch and position the rip fence so that the distance between it and the blade equals the width of the panel bevel—generally about 2 inches. Place the panel on the saw table facedown, one edge against the rip fence, and cut a groove in the panel face; make similar cuts parallel to the other three edges.

If you do not have a table saw, use a circular saw instead; clamp a guide to the panel to make straight cuts.

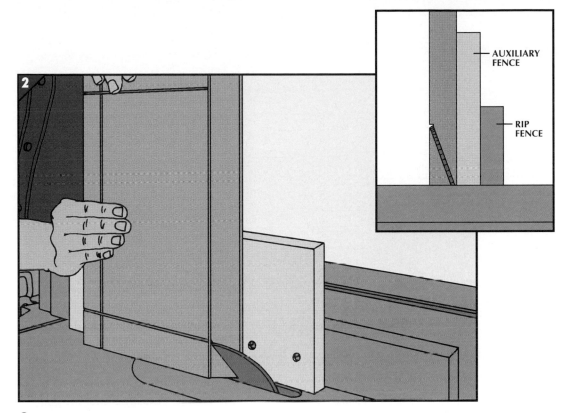

2. Cutting the bevel.

◆ Move the rip fence of the table saw to the left of the blade and secure a tall auxiliary fence to it *(page 18)*.

◆ Holding the panel with its back against the fence and its edge along the blade, adjust the fence position, blade projection, and blade tilt for a cut like that shown in the inset. The blade should enter the edge $\frac{3}{16}$ inch from the panel back and emerge from the front just below the cut made in the previous step.

◆ Keeping both hands well above the blade, slide the panel along the fence to cut the bevels around all four edges, then sand them so that they are smooth.

◆ Assemble the frame around the panel, gluing only the mortise-and-tenon joints to let the panel "float" inside the frame.

BEVELING BIT

BEVELING WITH A ROUTER

This beveling bit for a router, when run along the edge of a door panel, cuts the bevel shown at right. The protrusion at the bottom of the bevel fits into the dadoes in the door frame *(page 81)*. A beveling bit requires a variable-speed router set at a low speed, as recommended by the bit manufacturer. For best results, cut the bevel in several passes, increasing bit depth slightly with each pass.

CABINET HINGES

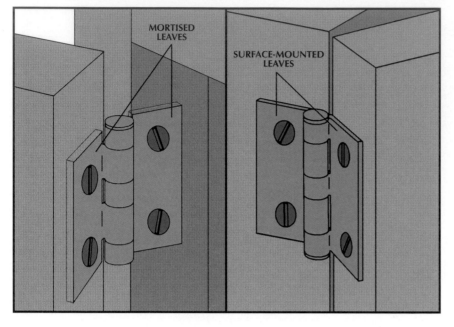

MORTISED LEAVES

SURFACE-MOUNTED LEAVES

Butt hinge.
For doors with frames of solid lumber, the hinge used most resembles those on house doors: two rectangular leaves that pivot on a central pin. Butt hinges can be used only on inset doors and on overlapping doors that cover the entire cabinet front. Install loose-pin butt hinges, which permit you to pull out the pin and remove the door without having to unscrew the leaves.

In the example at far left, the leaves of a butt hinge must be recessed, or mortised, into the cabinet's face frame and the edge of an inset door to allow room for the door to close within the frame; at near left, the leaves are installed without mortises on the side of the cabinet and the edge of an overlapping door.

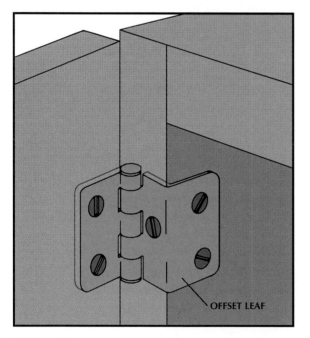

OFFSET LEAF

Offset hinge.
For cabinets made entirely of plywood—which does not securely hold screws set into its edges—offset hinges, sometimes called shutter hinges, permit fastening to the plywood faces, as in this overlapping door.

All offset hinges must be mortised rather than surface mounted; the offset leaf comes in various sizes to match standard plywood thicknesses.

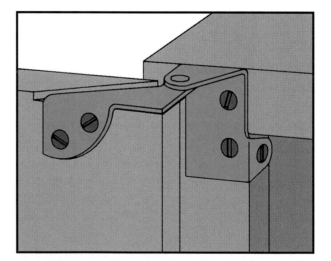

Pivot hinge.
More expensive than butt hinges and trickier to install, these "invisible hinges" are fitted to doors in a way that nearly or completely hides the hinge. Pivot hinges are installed in angled mortises at a door's top and bottom edges; when the door is closed, only a bit of the pivot is visible from the front.

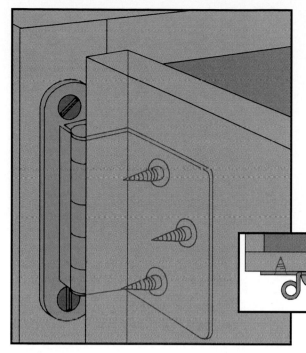

Semiconcealed hinge.

Designed for lipped and for partially overlapping doors, this hinge has one leaf surface mounted on the face of the cabinet and an offset leaf mortised into the back of the door. For the overlapping door in this example, the door leaf has an offset like that of a shutter hinge. On a lipped door *(inset)* the hinge has a double offset.

Buy the hinges for a lipped door before rabbeting the door, then rabbet the lip to a depth that matches the offset of the hinge.

DOUBLE OFFSET

FORSTNER BIT

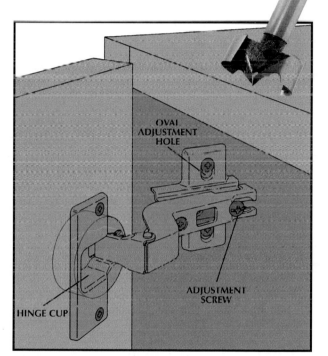

OVAL ADJUSTMENT HOLE

ADJUSTMENT SCREW

HINGE CUP

Euro-style hinge.

The cup on one leaf of this adjustable hinge fits in a $1\frac{3}{8}$-inch flat-bottomed cavity drilled in the door with a Forstner bit *(inset)*; the other leaf is screwed to the side of the cabinet. Oval holes in the cabinet leaf allow this hinge to move up and down on the mounting screws. In and out adjustments are accomplished by turning two screws in the hinge's center mechanism.

Euro-style hinges can be used only on overlapping or inset doors, and they come in two forms: one for frameless cabinets, often found in kitchens, and another for cabinets with face frames.

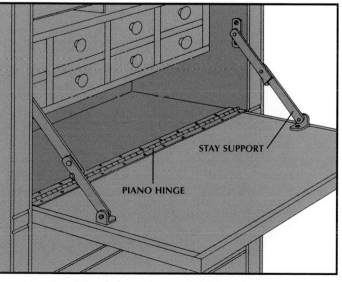

STAY SUPPORT

PIANO HINGE

Hardware for extra support.

On a very heavy door, and on a door like this fold-down work surface subjected to special strain when opened, mount a piano hinge—a surface-mounted butt hinge that runs the entire length of the door. Stay supports screwed to the cabinet and door relieve strain on the hinge. Such supports can also be used to limit the swing of a side-hinged door.

CATCHES AND LATCHES

Spring-action catch.
The arrow-shaped strike, mounted on the door, must be perfectly aligned with spring-loaded rollers mounted inside the cabinet. This assembly is especially durable and relatively quiet.

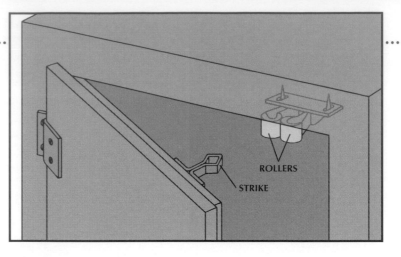

ROLLERS

STRIKE

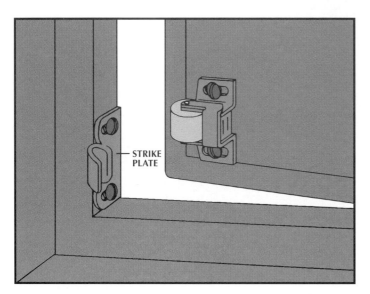

STRIKE PLATE

Single-roller catch.
The roller screwed to the door fits into a strike plate that is mounted on the cabinet. This catch is very quiet because it can be adjusted to prevent the door from striking the cabinet as it closes.

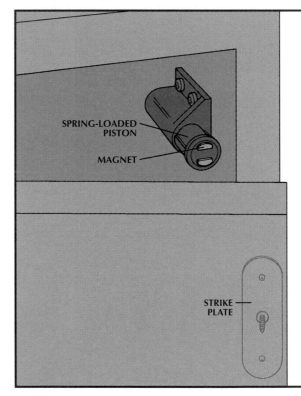

SPRING-LOADED PISTON

MAGNET

STRIKE PLATE

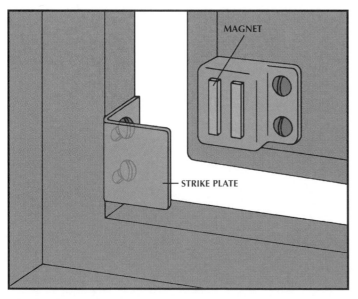

MAGNET

STRIKE PLATE

Magnetic catch.
A magnet in this catch grips a steel strike plate to hold the door closed. Above is a magnetic catch for a cabinet having a face frame; other models are available for frameless cabinets.

Touch catch.
This variation on the magnetic catch, intended for inset doors, is used as an alternative to a door handle. The strike plate on the door meets a magnet in a spring-loaded piston, which latches when the door is fully closed. Pressing on the door releases the latch, allowing the piston to push the door ajar.

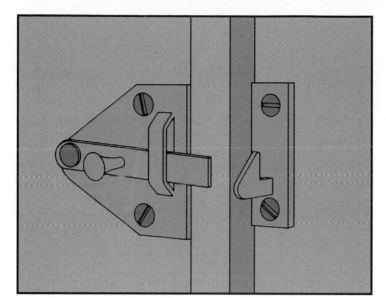

Bar latch.
An alternative to the various concealed catches is exterior hardware, such as a bar latch. This latch serves as a door pull as well as a catch.

HINGING OVERLAPPING DOORS

1. Installing hinges on the door.
◆ Position a hinge on the door so the pin is centered on the back edge (*right*). Outline the edge of the leaf and then drill pilot holes through the screw holes with a self-centering bit (*page 29*).
◆ Attach the hinge to the door and repeat for the other hinge or hinges.

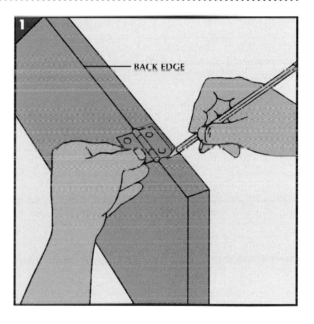

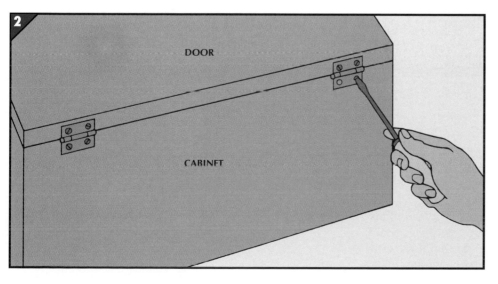

2. Attaching the door.
◆ Lay the cabinet on its back and fit the door over the opening.
◆ On the side of the cabinet, drill pilot holes as in Step 1.
◆ Screw the hinges to the cabinet.

HINGING INSET DOORS

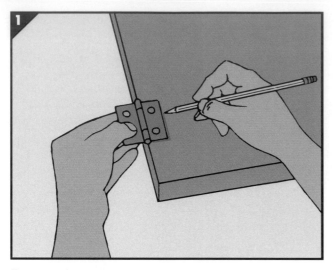

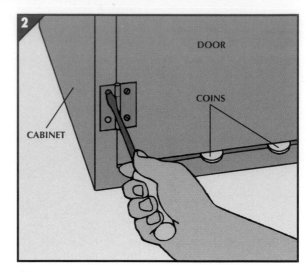

1. Installing hinges on the door.
◆ Align the leaf of one hinge on the front of the door so the pin is centered on the edge as shown above. Trace the outline of the leaf, then drill pilot holes through the screw holes with a self-centering bit. Be careful not to drill completely through the door.
◆ Attach the hinge to the door and repeat for the other hinge or hinges.

2. Attaching the door to the cabinet.
◆ With the cabinet upright, set the door into the opening, and wedge it in place with coins—quarters are $\frac{1}{8}$ inch thick—on all sides except the hinge side, where the door should fit against the frame.
◆ Drill pilot holes with a self-centering bit, then screw the hinges to the cabinet.

MORTISING HINGES ON OVERLAPPING DOORS

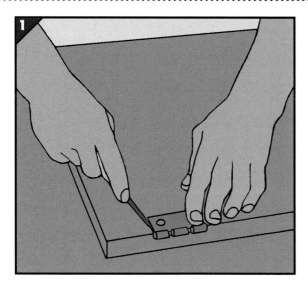

1. Marking the mortise.
◆ If your hinge has a removable pin, take it out; it is best to work with separated leaves.
◆ Place one leaf on the back of the door so that only the pin loops extend beyond the back edge. Outline the leaf with an awl (left).

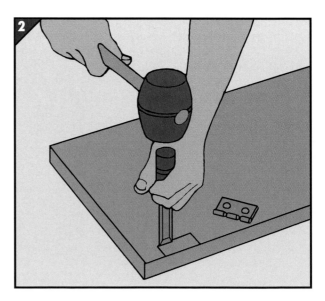

2. Cutting the mortise.
◆ Hold a chisel on the leaf outline and perpendicular to the door, with its beveled side toward the mortise area. Tap around the outline with the chisel and a mallet to make a small cut approximately the thickness of the hinge leaf.
◆ Hold the chisel beveled side down and at a low angle to the wood, then tap the chisel to make a series of short, shallow cuts, which make a smoother mortise than longer ones.
◆ Finish by using the chisel alone, bevel side up, to shave the entire mortise to the exact thickness of the hinge leaf.

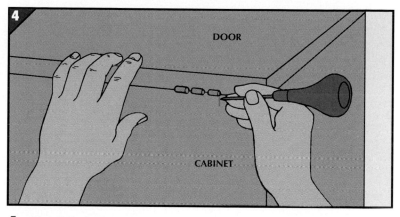

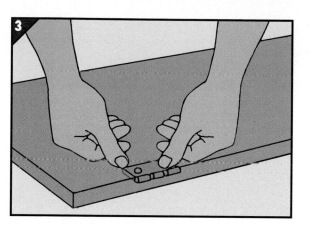

3. Checking the mortise.

◆ Place the hinge leaf in the mortise and align it so that only the pin loops extend beyond the edge of the door. Deepen the mortise or place a cardboard shim beneath the hinge as needed to bring the leaf flush with the door's face.

◆ Drill pilot holes with a self-centering bit, being careful not to drill completely through the door, then attach the leaf to the door. Mortise and attach the other hinge or hinges in the same way.

4. Attaching the door.

◆ Lay the cabinet on its back; fit the door over the opening.

◆ Mark the width of each attached hinge on the side of the cabinet *(above)*, then set the door aside.

◆ Using the marks for orientation, position the other hinge leaves on the front edge of the cabinet side and outline them with an awl. (If your hinges do not come apart, transfer the dimensions of the leaves to the cabinet edge with a combination square.)

◆ Cut mortises for the hinges within the outlines, drill pilot holes, and screw the leaves to the cabinet side.

◆ Set the door in place and reinsert the hinge pins.

MORTISING HINGES ON INSET DOORS

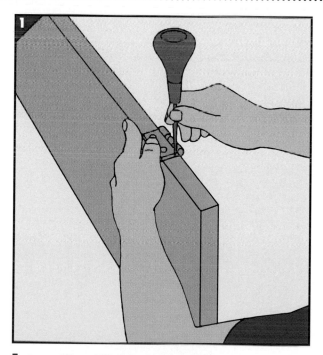

1. Installing hinges on the door.

On the side edge of the door, mortise the hinge leaves as shown in Steps 1 through 3 for mortising butt hinges on overlapping doors. Be sure the pin loops extend beyond the door's front edge *(above)*.

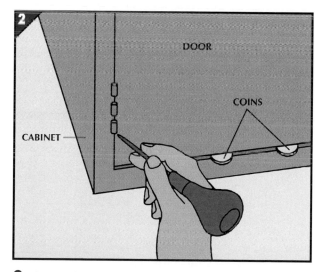

2. Attaching the door.

◆ With the cabinet upright, set the door into the opening; wedge it in place at the top and bottom with coins.

◆ Mark the tops and bottoms of the hinges on the cabinet's front edge *(above)*; set the door aside.

◆ Cut the mortises and install the hinges and door as explained in Step 4 at the top of this page.

Modular wall systems are a stylish solution to the problem of limited space and can be built for a fraction of the cost of ready-mades. Furthermore, you can easily put your own stamp on a homemade modular system by introducing features like a desk alcove with an overhanging bookcase *(pages 92-98)* or a cabinet shelf that will house a television set *(pages 99-101)*.

Infinite Adaptability: The system shown at right consists of two basic modules—a cabinet below and a bookcase above. Their simple design may be repeated again and again, their dimensions and details varied, but the result will always look sleek and well-balanced. Individual modules are screwed together for easy disassembly should you wish to rearrange elements or add new ones *(page 101)*.

Any type of cabinet will work as a base unit—the one constructed on pages 62 to 71 is suitable, though you may wish to omit the drawers and doors. For bookcases that rest on the cabinets, adapt the plan shown on pages 97 and 98 for a unit that bridges a space between two modules. In addition to making the bookcase taller, mimic the top of the structure at the bottom, replacing the double plywood base of the bridge unit with a single piece of plywood and cleats.

The Problems of Wiring: If any of the components of the modular system are to house electronic equipment, such as a television or stereo, you must drill exit holes through the units for wires and plugs. Plan carefully to minimize the number of holes.

A typical modular system.

The illustration below shows a trio of cabinet and book-case modules punctuated by a computer desk. The small bookcase above the desk keeps reference works within easy reach, and a sliding shelf below the desk holds a computer keyboard. Each cabinet is screwed to the one on its left, as well as to the wall for stability.

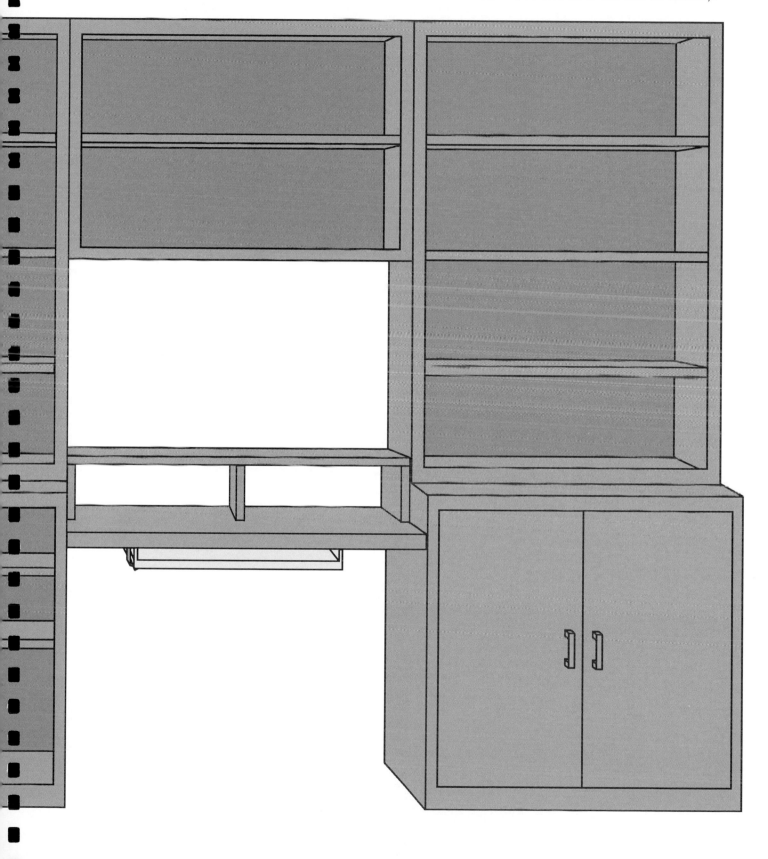

A Compact Computer Center

A computer desk sandwiched between modular units provides an efficient workspace that neatly punctuates a wall system. To make the most of the space—and better blend it with its surroundings—you can install a bookcase over the desk *(pages 97-98)*.

Useful Features: The desk consists of a writing surface topped by a low platform that holds the monitor of a personal computer. The platform is removable so the desk can be cleared for other uses, and the pigeonholes created by the platform supports can house the computer itself and a printer. A sliding keyboard shelf, available at computer-supply stores, hides the keyboard under the desk when the computer is not in use.

Desk Dimensions: The desk surface can be as deep as the neighboring cabinets or even a few inches deeper, to protrude a few inches beyond the cabinet fronts. For structural integrity, however, the desk should be no wider than 40 inches. The platform will be almost as wide as the desk, but its depth and height depend on the size of the computer. Measure your own computer monitor and other components for a custom fit. Finally, a comfortable height for the desktop is about 27 inches above the floor.

 TOOLS

Table saw or
  circular saw
Hammer
Electric drill
Tape measure
Screwdriver
Marking gauge
Awl

 **MATERIALS**

Hardwood plywood
  ($\frac{3}{4}$")
1 x 2
1 x 6 to 1 x 12 for
  platform supports
Glue *(page 37)*
Sandpaper (60-,
  100-, and
  150-grit)

Brads ($1\frac{1}{4}$")
Finishing nails ($1\frac{1}{2}$")
Retractable key-
  board shelf
Flat-head wood
  screws ($1\frac{1}{2}$" No.
  8, $1\frac{1}{4}$" No. 10,
  and 2" No. 10)

 **SAFETY TIPS**

Safety goggles protect your eyes when you are working with power tools, hammering, drilling, or sawing.

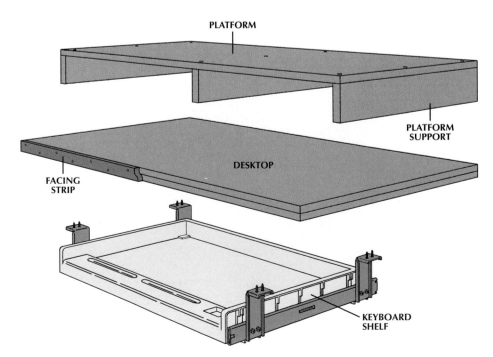

PLATFORM

PLATFORM
SUPPORT

DESKTOP

FACING
STRIP

KEYBOARD
SHELF

Plywood doubled for sturdiness.
Made from two layers of plywood, the desktop of this computer center is glued and nailed together with the higher quality side of the plywood exposed; a 1-by-2 facing strip finishes the desk's front edge. The platform, also of plywood and supported by three lengths of 1-inch lumber, rests on top of the desktop, while the sliding keyboard shelf hangs from the underside. The entire assembly spans a pair of 1-by-2 cleats screwed to the flanking cabinet modules *(page 96)*.

MAKING THE DESKTOP

1. Assembling the panels.
◆ Cut two plywood panels to the dimensions of the desk.
◆ Lay one of the panels, good side down, on a work surface padded as necessary to protect the wood. Squeeze parallel lines of glue 3 inches apart on the panel surface.
◆ Lay the second panel, its good side facing up, on top of the first. Align the edges and nail the two panels together with three rows of $1\frac{1}{4}$-inch brads driven at 4-inch intervals *(left)*.
◆ With a clean, damp cloth, wipe away any glue that seeps from between the panels.
◆ If one panel overhangs the other slightly because of imperfect measuring and cutting, sand the desktop edges to make them even.

FACING STRIP

2. Covering the front edge.
◆ Cut a 1-by-2 facing strip to the width of the desk.
◆ Apply a line of glue along the front edge of each desktop panel.
◆ Then lay the facing strip on the glue and align it with the edge of the desk.
◆ Nail the strip in place *(left)* with two staggered rows of $1\frac{1}{2}$-inch finishing nails, each row $\frac{3}{8}$ inch from an edge of the 1-by-2.
◆ If the facing strip projects beyond the desk's upper or lower surfaces, sand it down. Start with 60-grit sandpaper, then—to avoid marring the desk surface—switch to 100-grit, then 150-grit paper as the strip is brought flush with the desk.

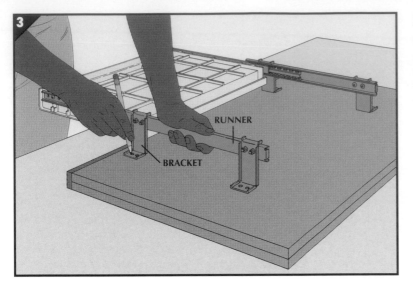

3. Fitting the keyboard shelf.

◆ Assemble the shelf according to the manufacturer's instructions. Typically, brackets need to be fastened to shelf runners.

◆ Place the desktop, nailheads up, on a work surface, then set the shelf, its runners fully extended, on the desk at the desired position. Mark the locations of the bracket mounting holes (left).

◆ Set the shelf aside and drill pilot holes for the mounting screws provided.

RUNNER

BRACKET

A PRINTER PLATFORM

1. Drilling platform screw holes.

◆ Cut the platform to the depth you wish and slightly shorter than the width of the desktop.

◆ On the good surface of the platform, draw pencil lines for the two end supports parallel to and $\frac{3}{8}$ inch from each end.

◆ Draw a third line at the location that is desired for the third support.

◆ Next, pencil three marks across each line—one at the midpoint, the others $1\frac{1}{2}$ inches from the front and back edges of the panel.

◆ Drill a $\frac{3}{16}$-inch hole through the platform at the marks, counterboring each hole for the head of a No. 8 flathead wood screw.

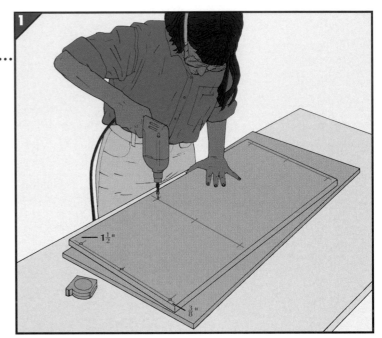

$1\frac{1}{2}$"

$\frac{3}{8}$"

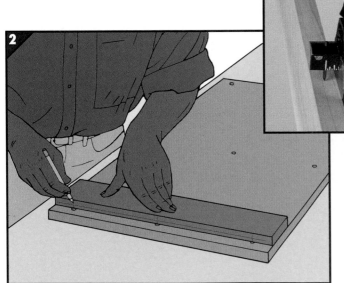

2. Marking the supports.

◆ From a 1-inch board up to 12 inches wide, cut three platform supports equal in length to the depth of the platform.

◆ With a marking gauge (inset), scribe a line down the center of one long edge of each of the supports.

◆ Lay one support flat on the underside of the platform, along a row of screw holes. Align the support ends with the panel edges. Pencil a mark on the edge of the support at the center of each hole (left).

◆ Number the support and its position on the panel in order to pair them again later.

◆ Repeat this procedure for the other two supports.

3. Completing the assembly.

◆ With a $\frac{3}{32}$-inch bit, drill $\frac{3}{4}$-inch-deep pilot holes in the supports at each mark *(right)*.

◆ Apply a thin line of glue to the drilled edge of each support, and fasten the pieces to the platform with $1\frac{1}{2}$-inch No. 8 flat-head wood screws.

◆ Cut a pair of 1-by-2 mounting cleats $\frac{3}{4}$ inch shorter than the depth of the cabinets that will support the desk. Mark the centerline of the face of each cleat 2 inches and 5 inches from each end, then drill a $\frac{1}{4}$-inch counterbored screw hole at each mark.

◆ Sand and finish the desktop, platform, and cleats *(pages 108-117)*.

◆ When the finish has dried, detach the keyboard-shelf brackets from the runners and screw the brackets to the underside of the desktop.

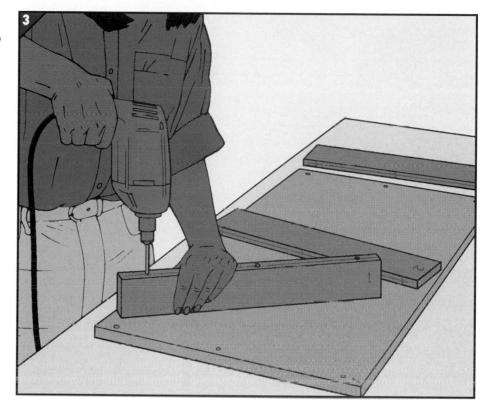

MOUNTING THE DESK

Marking guidelines.

◆ Mark a horizontal line across the side of each flanking cabinet at the desired height of the bottom edge of the desk *(right)*.

◆ Draw a second line $\frac{3}{8}$ inch above the first on each cabinet.

2. Marking for pilot holes.
◆ Holding a cleat with its front end $\frac{3}{4}$ inch back from a cabinet's face, align its upper edge with the lower pencil line.
◆ With an awl, mark through the holes in the cleat to indicate pilot-hole locations on the side of the cabinet *(left)*.
◆ Mark pilot-hole positions on the other cabinet with the other cleat.
◆ Drill a $\frac{1}{8}$-inch pilot hole, $\frac{5}{8}$ inch deep, at each awl mark.

3. Drilling upper screw holes.
◆ Directly above each pilot hole you made in Step 2, drill a $\frac{1}{4}$-inch hole through the cabinet sides along the upper pencil line *(right)*.
◆ Attach the cleats to the cabinets along the lower guidelines with $1\frac{1}{4}$-inch No. 10 flat-head wood screws.

4. Screwing the desk in place.
◆ Rest the desktop on the cleats, enlisting a helper if necessary to push the flanking cabinets snugly against the ends. Check the alignment of the desktop with the cabinets.
◆ From inside the cabinets, drill through the holes made in Step 3 with a $\frac{1}{8}$-inch bit, boring $1\frac{1}{4}$ inches into each end of the desk.
◆ Drive 2-inch No. 10 flat-head wood screws into the holes.
◆ Reattach the computer keyboard shelf to its brackets and set the platform on the desktop.

A Bookcase Accompaniment

Installing a bookcase over the desk unit on pages 92 to 96 encloses the desk in a snug niche and affords the user ready access to reference materials. The size of the bookcase is dictated by the dimensions of the flanking modules and the desk. It must be as wide as the desk, no deeper than the modules, and short enough to leave space for the computer monitor that sits atop the desk platform. Measure the space carefully before cutting the wood.

Easy Installation: Because of its considerable weight, the bookcase is installed in a way that requires lifting it only once *(page 98, Step 3)*. To use this technique, you will need two pieces of 1-by-3 or other strong scrap wood, each at least a foot wider than the bookcase, to use as temporary supports. Once in place above the desk, the bookcase is anchored by screws driven into its sides from inside the neighboring modules.

 TOOLS

Hammer	Combination drill
Pencil or awl	bits
Screwdriver	Table saw or
Electric drill	circular saw

 **MATERIALS**

Plywood	Brads (1" and $1\frac{1}{4}$")
($\frac{3}{4}$" and $\frac{1}{4}$")	Flat-head screws
1 x 2s	($1\frac{1}{2}$" No. 8 and
1 inch lumber	$1\frac{1}{4}$" No. 8)
Parting bead	Shelf pins
Glue *(page 37)*	

 **SAFETY TIPS**

Safety goggles protect your eyes when you are working with power tools, hammering, drilling, and sawing.

A place for books.

This bookcase consists of a plywood box with 1-by-2 reinforcing cleats at the top and a double, lipped bottom to support the sides. Box edges are concealed behind a 1-by-2 face frame *(pages 66-71)*; the edge of an adjustable shelf, which can rest on pins as shown here or on other kinds of supports *(pages 50-51)*, is hidden by a strip of parting bead. Top, sides, and bottom are made of $\frac{3}{4}$-inch hardwood plywood, while the back uses $\frac{1}{4}$-inch stock.

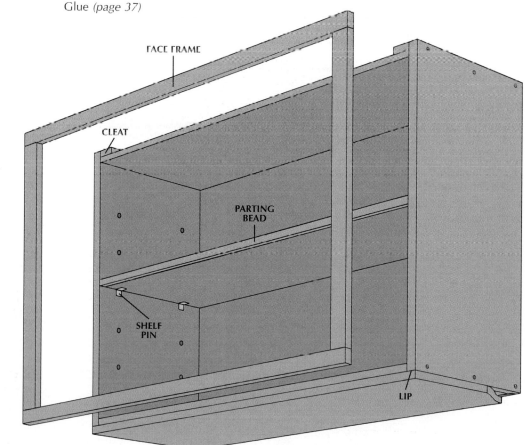

FACE FRAME

CLEAT

PARTING BEAD

SHELF PIN

LIP

BRIDGING BETWEEN MODULES

1. Assembling the bottom.

◆ Cut two plywood panels, one the width and depth of the bookcase, the other $1\frac{1}{2}$ inches narrower and $\frac{3}{8}$ inch shallower.

◆ Lay the larger panel, good side down, on a worktable. Place the smaller one on top of the larger, centered left to right and flush with a long edge, then outline the smaller piece with a pencil.

◆ Remove the smaller piece, and squeeze parallel beads of glue at 2-inch intervals between the lines.

◆ Replace the smaller piece, good side up, and press it against the glue.

◆ Drive three rows of $1\frac{1}{4}$-inch brads through the smaller panel into the larger.

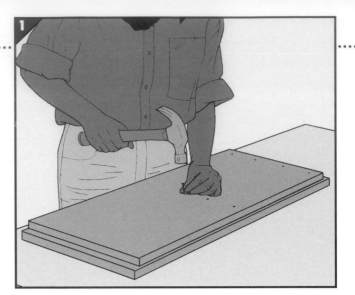

2. Building the case.

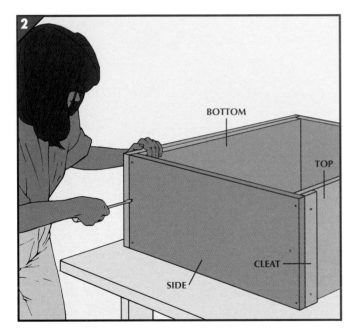

◆ Make a top panel the same size as the smaller bottom panel and fasten a 1-by-2 cleat, cut to the depth of the top, at each end with glue and $1\frac{1}{4}$-inch brads.

◆ Cut bookcase sides the same depth as the top and notch each with a $\frac{3}{8}$-inch rabbet to accept the back panel. With a drilling jig (page 51), bore holes in the sides for shelf-support pins.

◆ Align a side panel with the top, counterbore three pilot holes through the side into the cleat, and screw the side to the cleat with $1\frac{1}{2}$-inch No. 8 flat-head screws. Repeat for the other side.

◆ Set the assembly into the lipped bottom; fasten the sides to the ends of the smaller panel with $1\frac{1}{2}$-inch No. 8 screws (left).

◆ Make a back as wide as the smaller bottom panel and $1\frac{1}{2}$ inches shorter than a side. Fit it into the side rabbets and the lipped bottom. Attach the back with glue and 1-inch brads.

◆ Construct a face frame from 1-by-2s and attach it to the case (pages 66-71).

◆ Cut a plywood shelf $\frac{1}{4}$ inch narrower than the distance between the sides and 1 inch shallower. Attach parting bead to the front edge with glue and brads.

3. Installing the unit.

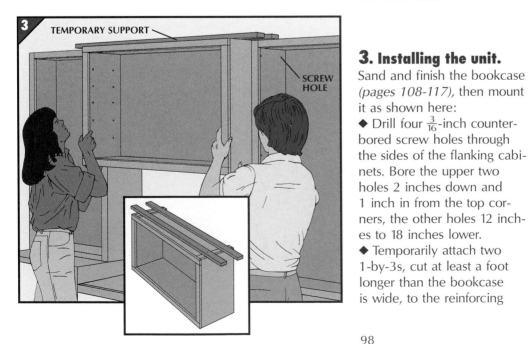

Sand and finish the bookcase (pages 108-117), then mount it as shown here:

◆ Drill four $\frac{3}{16}$-inch counterbored screw holes through the sides of the flanking cabinets. Bore the upper two holes 2 inches down and 1 inch in from the top corners, the other holes 12 inches to 18 inches lower.

◆ Temporarily attach two 1-by-3s, cut at least a foot longer than the bookcase is wide, to the reinforcing cleats, using $1\frac{1}{4}$-inch-long No. 8 screws (inset).

◆ With a helper, hang the bookcase unit between two modules (left), then align all three units.

◆ Drill $\frac{3}{32}$-inch pilot holes, $\frac{1}{2}$ inch deep, into the bookcase through the screw holes in the cabinets.

◆ Fasten the units together with $1\frac{1}{4}$-inch No. 8 flat-head screws driven from inside the cabinets.

◆ Remove the 1-by-3s from the top of the bookcase.

TOOLS

Hammer
Electric drill
Pencil or awl
Circular saw
Pliers or wrenches
Screwdriver

MATERIALS

Plywood ($\frac{3}{4}$")
1-by-4 for glide supports
Glue (page 37)
Shelf glides
Turntable
Round-head wood screws
  ($1\frac{1}{4}$" No. 8 and $\frac{5}{8}$" No. 6)
Machine screws ($\frac{3}{16}$" x $1\frac{1}{2}$"),
  with washers and nuts

SAFETY TIPS

Safety goggles protect your eyes when you are working with power tools, hammering, drilling, and sawing.

A particularly useful way to customize a cabinet module is the television platform shown below. The key elements in the television cabinet are a lazy Susan-style turntable and heavy-duty metal shelf glides. Both are available through hardware stores and mail-order specialty houses; the glides are often sold specifically as television shelf glides. Assembled with two plywood panels, these parts make a slide-out, rotating shelf that can support a television of modest size.

Providing Extra Support: To prevent the television from tipping the cabinet over when the shelf is pulled out, screw the cabinet through its back into at least one wall stud. If there is a baseboard, or if you need to leave space behind the unit for an electrical cord, screw the unit to the wall through a spacing board. And to further stabilize the system, screw neighboring units together to form a single structure against the wall *(page 101)*.

A movable shelf.

This double shelf is made from two pieces of $\frac{3}{4}$-inch plywood joined by a turntable. The entire assembly slides in and out of the cabinet on glides fitted to the lower shelf and screwed to 1-by-4 cleats fixed to the sides of the cabinet. To conceal the television when it is not in use, add doors to the cabinet *(pages 78 89)*.

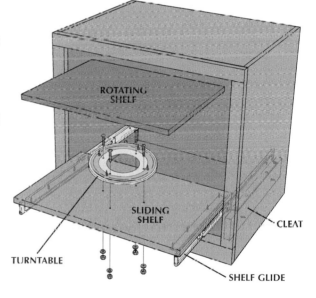

A SLIDING, ROTATING SHELF

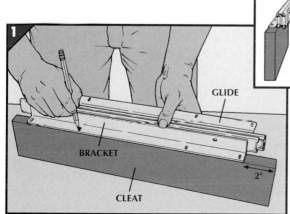

1. Preparing the cleats.

◆ Cut two cleats to the interior depth of the cabinet.
◆ Mark the top edge of each cleat 2 inches from one end. Position a shelf glide on a cleat as shown at left and mark screw-hole locations through the mounting bracket. Repeat for the other cleat, noting that one glide is intended for the left side of the shelf, the other for the right side *(inset)*.
◆ Drill $\frac{3}{32}$-inch pilot holes at the marks, and attach the glides with the screws provided.
◆ Set each cleat on the cabinet floor, against the side, then drill two $\frac{3}{32}$-inch pilot holes through the cleat and $\frac{3}{8}$ inch into the side.
◆ Coat the cleats with glue, and screw them in place with $1\frac{1}{4}$-inch No. 8 round-head wood screws.

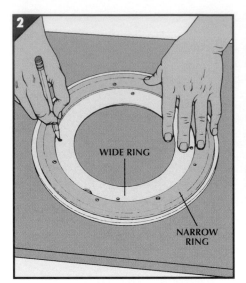

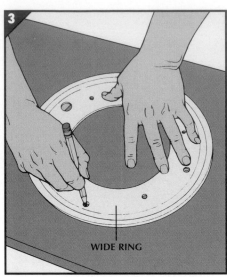

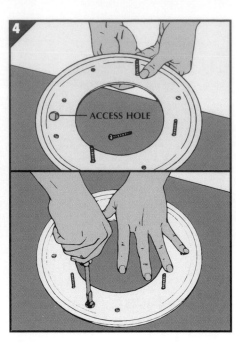

2. Holes in the sliding shelf.

◆ Cut a sliding shelf to the interior depth of the cabinet and $\frac{1}{2}$ inch narrower than the cabinet opening.

◆ Lay the shelf on a work surface, good side up. Center the turntable on the shelf with the wide ring down.

◆ Mark the shelf through the four visible small holes in the wide ring. Set the turntable aside and drill $\frac{1}{4}$-inch holes through the shelf at the marks.

3. Drilling the rotating shelf.

◆ Cut another shelf to the same depth as the sliding shelf but 4 inches narrower.

◆ Lay the shelf on the work surface, good side down. Center the turntable on it, narrow ring down.

◆ Turn the wide ring to align the four medium-sized edge holes with the four smallest holes in the narrow ring. Mark the shelf through the holes.

◆ Set the turntable aside; bore $\frac{3}{32}$-inch pilot holes $\frac{5}{8}$ inch deep at the marks.

◆ Apply a finish to the shelves (pages 108-117).

4. Mounting the turntable.

◆ With the wide ring up, insert $\frac{3}{16}$-inch round-head machine screws, $1\frac{1}{2}$ inches long, through its four small holes (above, top).

◆ Rotate the wide ring so its large access hole is over a small mounting hole in the narrow ring. Position both holes over a pilot hole in the rotating shelf, and drive a $\frac{5}{8}$-inch No. 6 round-head screw there (above, bottom).

◆ Turning the wide ring as necessary, drive screws through the remaining mounting holes in the narrow ring.

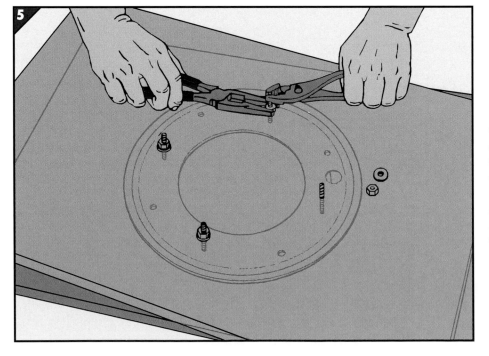

5. Attaching the sliding shelf.

◆ Lower the sliding shelf, good side down, onto the machine screws in the turntable.

◆ Secure the shelf with washers and nuts. While holding the tip of each screw with pliers, tighten its nut with a second pair of pliers or with a small wrench (left).

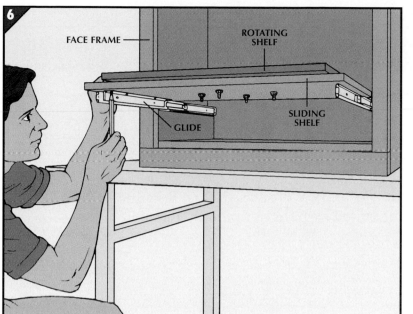

FACE FRAME

ROTATING SHELF

GLIDE

SLIDING SHELF

6. Mounting the turntable assembly.

◆ Push the glides all the way into the cabinet, then set the turntable assembly on top of them.

◆ Center the assembly on the glides with the front edge resting just behind the face frame. Then, without disturbing the assembly on the glides, extend them fully.

◆ Mark screw-hole locations on the underside of the sliding shelf through the holes in the extended glides *(left)*.

◆ Lift the shelf assembly from the glides and drill pilot holes at the marks for the screws provided.

◆ Screw the assembly to the extended glides.

◆ Through either the back or the side of the cabinet, drill a hole large enough for the plug to pass through.

◆ Apply a finish to the cabinet, removing shelf and glides, if necessary, for better access.

JOINING CABINET MODULES

Connecting upper and lower modules.

◆ Make two marks on the top of the lower module, each $1\frac{1}{2}$ inches in from a side and $3\frac{1}{2}$ inches in from the back. Make two additional marks, each $1\frac{1}{2}$ inches in from a side and $1\frac{1}{2}$ inches in from where the front edge of the upper module will lie.

◆ Drill a $\frac{3}{32}$-inch pilot hole through the top at each mark.

◆ Place the upper unit atop the lower one.

◆ Drill through each pilot hole with a $\frac{3}{32}$-inch bit until you have drilled $\frac{1}{2}$ inch into the upper unit.

◆ Drive a $1\frac{1}{4}$-inch No. 8 round-head wood screw into each hole *(left)*.

Neighboring modules.

◆ Where two modules abut, drill four $\frac{3}{16}$-inch counterbored holes through the side of one of them. Space the holes 3 inches from the top, 5 inches from the bottom, and 2 inches from the front and back.

◆ Push the units together. Drilling through the holes, bore $\frac{3}{32}$-inch pilot holes $\frac{5}{8}$ inch deep into the neighboring unit *(right)*.

◆ Join the modules with $1\frac{1}{4}$-inch No. 8 flat-head wood screws.

Finishing Touches

The undisguised boxiness of bookcases and cabinets may fit in perfectly with some settings, but elsewhere the squarish lines can clash with the decor. When that happens—or whenever you want to modestly embellish a cabinet—you can add moldings to soften some of the right angles. Applying a finish, often preceded by staining the wood, is the final step that brings the piece to life.

Dressing Up the Finished Piece   **104**

Applying Base Molding
Adding Cap Molding
Cutting Special Joints

Smoothing the Surface   **108**

Selecting an Abrasive
Types of Sanders

Filling Wood for Sheen and Color   **110**

Staining Richness into Wood   **112**

Stain Types
Alcohol Stain
Oil Stains

Penetrating Oils   **114**

A Hard-Wearing Finish   **116**

A Solvent-Based Polyurethane Finish

Brushing on stain →

The difference between simple, modern-looking bookcases or cabinets and furniture with a more traditional flavor may be nothing more than the addition of wood moldings around the base or top of the piece. Molding also hides large nail or screw holes, eliminating the need for extensive wood filling and sanding, and it can conceal less-than-perfect artisanship at joints that the molding covers.

Wall units of the kind shown on pages 90 to 101 acquire a more unified appearance when they are fitted with baseboard molding along the bottom, vertical trim molding between modules, and crown molding at the ceiling.

Plan Ahead: Molding rarely succeeds as an afterthought. As you develop a design for your cabinet, examine samples of molding at a lumberyard to familiarize yourself with sizes and styles. Molding, unlike other types of lumber, is labeled at its actual dimensions. If you own a router, consider the many different router bits and the profiles they form to create your own molding from lumber ripped to size.

After choosing the moldings, incorporate them in the plans for the piece you are building as you draw them up. For example, design a top overhang of the correct depth to accommodate the bed molding you choose. On cabinets, modify the dimension of the kick space if you want to trim the bottom with molding, or omit the kick space.

Molding Basics: Attach moldings with small finishing nails, countersunk into the wood and covered with a dab of wood putty. Use the special joints shown on page 107 to prevent gaps as molding expands and contracts slightly with temperature and humidity changes.

 TOOLS

Backsaw and   Hammer
  miter box   Nail set
C clamps   Coping saw

 **MATERIALS**

Trim molding   Finishing nails
Ogee molding   ($1\frac{1}{2}$" and 2")
Bed molding   Brads (1")
Glue *(page 37)*

 **SAFETY TIPS**

A poorly aimed hammer blow can cause a partially driven nail to fly into your face. Protect your eyes with goggles.

Dressing up with moldings.

In the bookcase at right, shown with its face frame removed for clarity, bed molding joins the top to the sides and front. At the bottom, a combination of 1-inch trim molding capped with ogee molding embellishes the base. All the molding pieces meet at corner joints with 45-degree miter cuts *(opposite)*. Because the bed molding shown here does not lie flat against the bookcase, it must have a compound miter cut for the joints to fit properly.

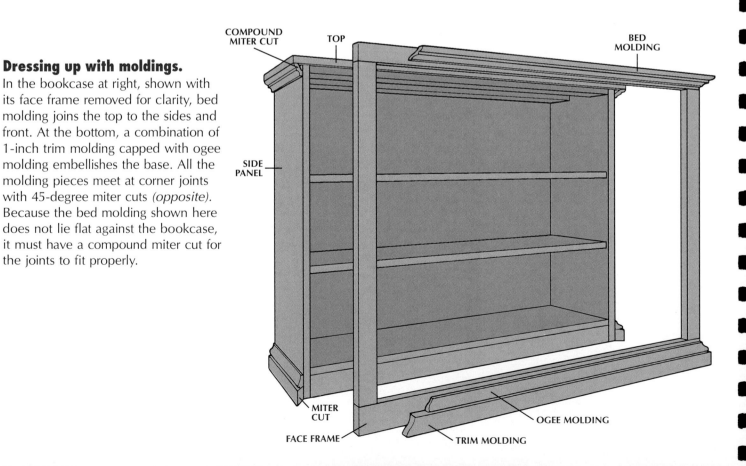

COMPOUND MITER CUT

TOP

BED MOLDING

SIDE PANEL

MITER CUT

FACE FRAME

OGEE MOLDING

TRIM MOLDING

APPLYING BASE MOLDING

1. Cutting trim in a miter box.
◆ Cut a piece of trim molding 4 inches longer than the front of the bookcase or cabinet.
◆ Place the piece of molding in a miter box, narrow side up. With a backsaw, cut the trim molding at a 45-degree angle, about 2 inches from one end *(right)*.

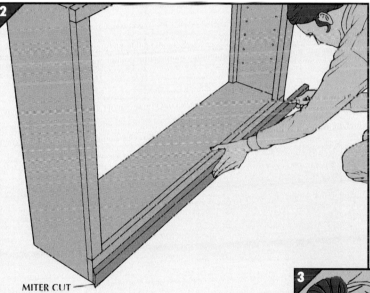

MITER CUT

2. Fitting the mitered trim.
◆ Align the mitered end of the molding with one corner of the bookcase and mark the top edge of the trim where it meets the other corner *(left)*.
◆ Make a 45-degree cut at the mark, orienting the workpiece in the miter box so that this cut will be opposite the first, picture-frame fashion.
◆ Fasten the trim to the bookcase with glue and $1\frac{1}{2}$ inch finishing nails, taking care to align the miter cuts with the corners of the bookcase. Sink the nailheads with a nail set.

3. Attaching side trim.
◆ Cut a piece of trim molding at least 4 inches longer than the side of the bookcase. Miter one end as described in Step 1.
◆ Hold the trim against the side of the bookcase, fitting the miter cut against the corresponding miter cut of the front trim.
◆ Mark the side trim where it meets the back corner of the bookcase, and use the miter box to cut a square end on the molding at the mark.
◆ Apply glue to the back of the trim, butt the mitered corners together, then secure the trim with $1\frac{1}{2}$-inch finishing nails. Sink the nailheads with a nail set.

4. Applying ogee molding.

◆ Measure and miter-cut ogee molding to fit the front of the bookcase as shown in Steps 1 and 2 on page 105.

◆ Apply glue to the back of the molding and set it atop the trim molding, aligned with the bookcase's corners.

◆ Drive 1-inch brads into the middle of the molding at a slight downward angle. Sink the heads of the brads with a nail set *(inset)*.

◆ Cut and fit the side pieces of ogee molding using the same techniques described in Step 3 on page 105.

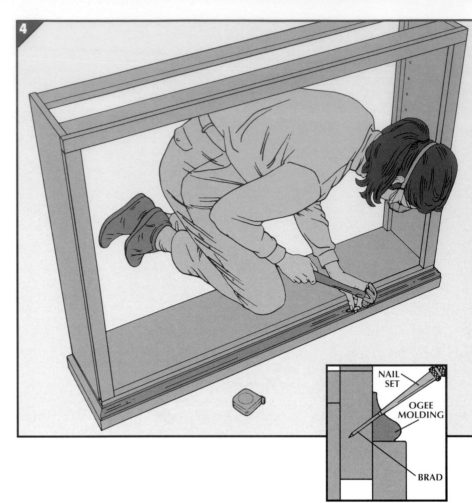

ADDING CAP MOLDING

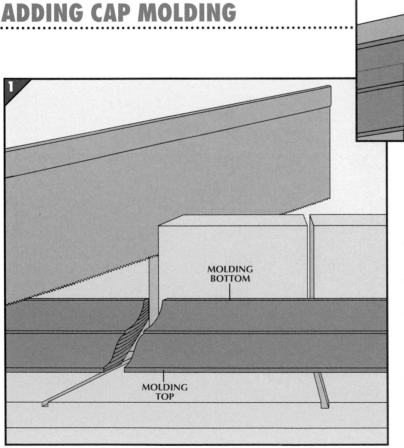

1. Dealing with bed molding.

For a correct fit, the molding around the top of the bookcase must be placed in the miter box upside down with respect to its future orientation. Bed moldings fit a miter box differently from trim and ogee moldings. After marking this type of molding for the front and sides of the cabinet *(page 105)*, position it against the back and bottom of the miter box as shown at left to make the compound miter joint that is illustrated in the inset.

2. Applying bed molding.

◆ Rest the bookcase upside down on scrap wood.

◆ Apply glue to the front molding and set it against the face frame and the underside of the top overhang, aligned with the corners of the bookcase.

◆ Drive 1 inch brads at an angle into the bookcase, sinking the heads with a nail set *(inset)*.

◆ Repeat the procedure for the side molding pieces.

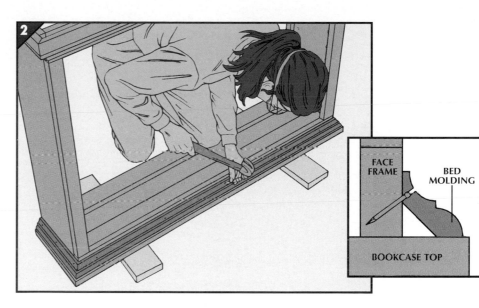

CUTTING SPECIAL JOINTS

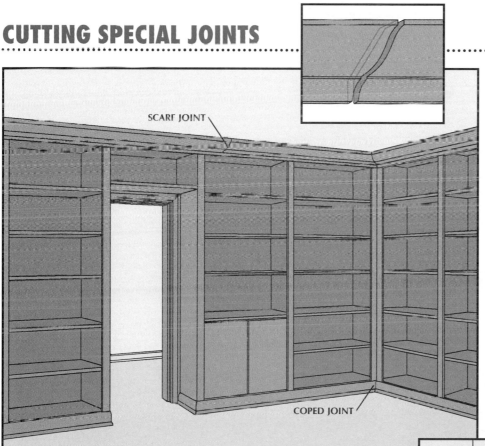

SCARF JOINT

COPED JOINT

Fashioning a scarf joint.

Where two lengths of molding meet end to end *(left)*, cut a scarf joint.

◆ Butt a length of molding in the corner, then cut off the opposite end at a 45-degree angle. Secure it to the bookcase with glue and finishing nails.

◆ Cut parallel miters on both ends of the next piece to slip under the miter on the preceding piece, unless it reaches to a corner with an adjacent wall. In that situation, cut one end of the piece at a 45-degree angle, then square-cut the other end to fit the corner.

◆ Glue the mitered ends together. Drive two 2-inch finishing nails through the overlapping miters of the scarf joint.

Coping an inside corner.

A coped joint *(inset, near right)* neatly compensates for a corner that is not quite square.

◆ Trim a piece of molding square on one end and butt it into the corner.

◆ Stand the adjoining piece on edge in a miter box and cut the end at a 45-degree angle. Run a pencil along the curved edge, or profile, of the cut to make it more visible.

◆ With a coping saw cut vertically along the pencil mark *(inset, far right)*. The molding now fits against the face of the piece already set into the corner.

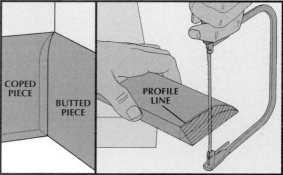

Smoothing the Surface

Before wood receives a finish, the surface must be carefully smoothed: If roughness or blemishes are not removed, they will be emphasized by the finish, not concealed. The smoothing is done in stages, using abrasives of progressively increasing fineness. Abrasives are also needed when the finish is applied—to create microscopic scratches in intermediate coats so that the next coat will adhere well, for example, or to reduce the luster of the final coat.

Abrasive Choices: Sandpaper and steel wool are the two main kinds of abrasives for wood. Both come in several grades, designed for the various purposes listed in the chart below. Steel wool, available only in fine textures, is preferred by many woodworkers for delicate jobs. Sandpaper, whose grit numbers refer to the size of its particles, is suited to the full range of smoothing tasks.

Sanding Tactics: If the wood is badly nicked or scratched, begin with 80-grit paper; otherwise start with 120-grit paper. Proceed to 150- or 180-grit, then 220. Do not try to work out a stubborn scratch by continuous rubbing with a fine grit; use coarse or medium paper to remove the defect, then repeat all grit levels to get back to where you left off.

The wood's grain should be raised before its final smoothing and application of the finish. Lightly wet the wood with a spray bottle, let it dry, then sand away the resulting whiskery fibers with 320-grit paper.

Removing Dust: Because the slightest trace of sawdust will spoil a finish, clean the surface with a vacuum cleaner and soft-bristled brush after each step of the smoothing process. Before you apply finish, wipe the surface clean, using a tack cloth if the finish will be solvent-based, or a wetted cloth if it will be water-based *(box, opposite).*

SAFETY TIPS *Goggles and a dust mask protect your eyes and lungs from the fine dust and grit created by sanding.*

Selecting an Abrasive

Sandpaper Type	Grit	Uses
Coarse	60, 80	Leveling deep depressions and scratches.
Medium	100, 120	Leveling shallow depressions and scratches.
Fine	150, 180	Final sanding of bare wood if a hard finish such as enamel or polyurethane is being used. Light sanding of intermediate coats of paint or polyurethane to promote adhesion and remove trapped particles and air bubbles.
Very Fine	220, 240	Final sanding of bare wood, unless grain will be raised. Light sanding of primer or sealer coats.
Extra Fine	280, 320, 360	Final sanding of bare wood if grain is raised. Sanding of intermediate coats of finish.
Super Fine	400, 600	Reducing luster of a high-gloss finish.

Steel Wool Type	Grade	Uses
Fine	2/0 (00)	Reducing luster of a high-gloss finish.
Extra Fine	3/0 (000)	Final smoothing of wood before applying finish. Abrading intermediate coats of finish. Lightly reducing luster of a high-gloss finish.
Super Fine	4/0 (0000)	Applying rubbing stain, wax, or oil. Abrading intermediate finish coats. Lightly reducing luster of a high-gloss finish.

TYPES OF SANDERS

Sanding block.

Sanding blocks are available at most hardware stores, but you can easily make your own. Cut from a piece of wood a block that will comfortably fit in the palm of your hand, about 3 inches square. Saw a slot $\frac{1}{8}$ inch deep along one edge. Sand sharp corners to round them slightly. Glue thick felt or smooth rubber onto both sides of the block.

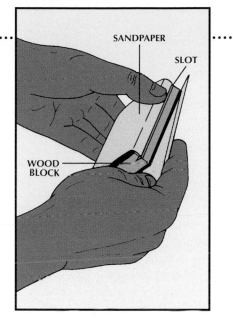

Cut a sheet of sandpaper large enough to wrap all the way around the block, plus $\frac{1}{4}$ inch. Insert one edge of the sandpaper into the slot, fold the sheet around the block *(right)*, and tuck the other end into the slot.

Apply moderate pressure, and work in the direction of the grain with long, even strokes.

Orbital sander.

The motor of an orbital sander moves sandpaper in a tight elliptical pattern at high speed. A variation of this tool, called a random-orbit sander, sands in an irregular pattern, lessening the potential of whorls in the wood. With either type, there is no need to sand exclusively with the grain.

Grip both handles of the sander firmly and switch on the motor before placing the sandpaper against the wood. Apply only gentle pressure; let the sander do the work as you move the tool in smooth back-and-forth passes. Keep the sander flat near the edges to avoid rounding them. Remove the sander from the wood before turning off the motor.

A Sander Designed for Corners

A power tool called a detail sander has a triangular head that vibrates only a few millimeters from side to side. This small motion and the pointed front make it ideal for sanding into tight corners inaccessible to a sanding block or orbital sander. An adhesive back holds the sanding pad firmly in place. Replaceable pads of various grits are available from the tool manufacturer or at most hardware stores.

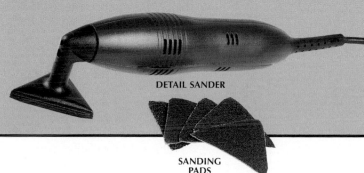

DETAIL SANDER

SANDING PADS

A HOMEMADE TACK CLOTH

A tack cloth, used to clean sawdust from a surface when applying solvent-based finishes, can be purchased at most hardware or paint stores, but you can also make your own. Lightly soak a lint-free cloth with mineral spirits, then add a few drops of varnish and knead the cloth to work the varnish throughout the fabric until it feels sticky. Add a few drops of varnish when it begins to lose its tackiness.

If your finish is water-based, wipe away dust with a piece of soft, lint-free cloth that has been moistened with water.

Filling Wood for Sheen and Color

When wood is sawed or planed, surface pores are created as the blade slices through hollow cells that carried fluids in the living tree. With close-grained woods like pine and fir, the pores are so small that a sealer such as shellac will fill them, yielding a smooth surface. Other woods—oak, ash, walnut, mahogany, and birch, for example—have larger pores alternating with dense, non-porous areas if the wood has a pronounced grain. Applying a filler to these large-pored woods helps produce a uniform smoothness.

Color Options: A filler with color added can heighten the contrast between open-pored wood and dense areas. Apply stain first, so it does not loosen or dissolve the filler; then, unless the filler color matches the stain, coat with a thin wash of shellac to prevent the stain and filler from smudging. For higher contrast, use a filler that is lighter than the stain; for a more natural appearance, use a filler at least as dark as the stain.

Most paint stores stock fillers in neutral shades and a few colors; more colors are available from woodworking suppliers. You can create a custom color by adding stain to a neutral filler. Make sure the stain is compatible with the filler; do not mix alcohol-based spirit stain with oil-based filler. Add the stain to the filler a little at a time, testing it on a hidden part of the piece that is made of the featured wood; add more filler or stain to adjust the color.

Types of Filler: Fillers used to smooth pores come in paste form, which must be diluted with turpentine or with mineral spirits, or as an already-thinned liquid. Both types must be thoroughly mixed before they can be used; when thinning a paste filler, add the recommended solvent, stirring constantly, until the mixture has the consistency of thick cream.

An altogether different kind of product, also called wood filler, is used to fill nail or screw holes and the rough edges of particle board and plywood. This kind of filler—a putty or spackling compound—is applied with a putty knife. Pack it into holes and coat the surface with a layer about $\frac{1}{16}$ inch thick. Allow the filler to dry overnight, then sand the surface smooth with 150-grit sandpaper. Apply more of the filler if the dried coat has shrunk beneath the surface.

 TOOLS

Mixing jars or cans
Mixing sticks
Synthetic-bristle
   paintbrush
Paintbrush with 2"
   stiff bristles
Burlap

 **MATERIALS**

Wood filler
Shellac
Denatured alcohol
Stain for filler
Sandpaper (220-
   and 400-grit)

SAFETY TIPS

Rubber or vinyl gloves protect your hands while mixing and applying stains and fillers. Always work in a well-ventilated area when using alcohol- or spirit-based fillers and finishes.

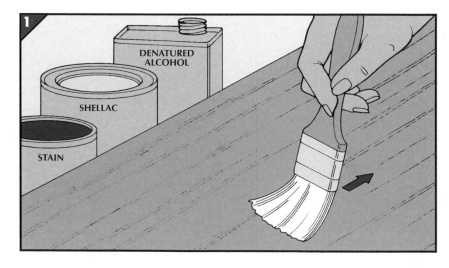

1. Applying a shellac wash coat.
If you are using a filler of a different color from the stain, prepare and apply a shellac wash coat after the stain and before the filler.
◆ Dilute the shellac with 8 parts of denatured alcohol to 1 part of shellac.
◆ With a synthetic-bristle paintbrush, apply the wash along the grain in a thin coat, let it dry for 30 minutes, and sand the surface lightly with 220-grit sandpaper. Take care not to sand all the way through the shellac coat.

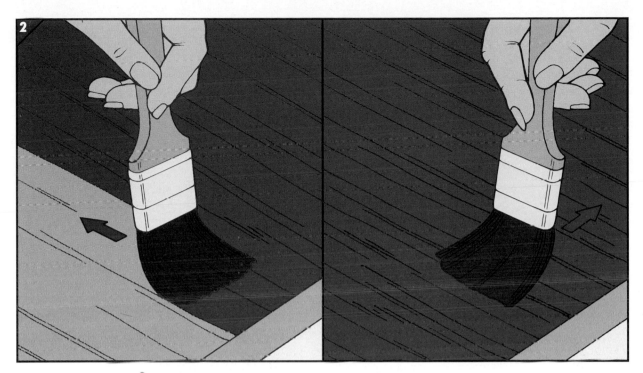

2. Applying wood filler.
◆ Mix the filler with a clean stick, adding stain and solvent in small amounts to achieve the proper color and consistency.
◆ With a paintbrush with stiff bristles about 2 inches long, apply liberal amounts of filler, pressing it into the pores of the wood. First brush in the direction of the grain *(above, left)*, then across it *(above, right)*, until a thick coating of filler covers the surface.
◆ Allow the filler to set until it congeals and loses its gloss, but do not let it dry completely before padding *(below)*.

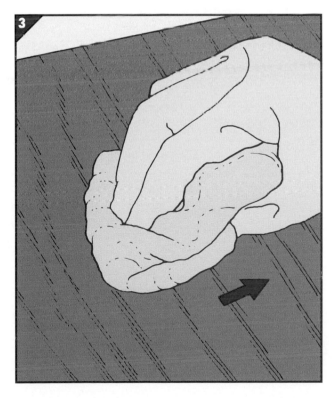

3. Padding the filler.
◆ Using a pad of folded burlap, rub the filler across the grain, applying moderate pressure to fill the pores completely and remove the excess.
◆ Lightly wipe along the grain to clean the surface. Let the filler dry for at least 24 hours (more time may be needed in cold or humid conditions).
◆ Shine a light across the grain to make sure the pores are filled. If you do not see a slight sheen, or if you see varying highlights and flat areas, brush on and pad a second coat.
◆ When the final coat is completely dry, sand it smooth with 400-grit sandpaper before applying the finish.

Staining Richness into Wood

Wood stains vary not only in color but also in their composition. The various types, along with their advantages and disadvantages, are described in the chart below. Oil-based stains are the most widely available; stains based on other solvents are sold at paint stores that serve furniture makers.

Oil Stains: Stains with an oil base come in two classes. Penetrating-oil stains carry transparent dyes in solution; the dyes are absorbed by the wood fibers and thus color the wood without creating a surface film. Nonpenetrating-oil stains, which are also called pigmented wiping stains, contain pigments in suspension and act by depositing color on the wood fibers rather than soaking into them.

Some oil stains carry both dyes and pigments. This kind of stain must be mixed well and handled the same as a nonpenetrating stain.

Other Stains: Alcohol stains are sold either as powdered dye, to be mixed with denatured alcohol, or as premixed liquids. So-called "non-grain-raising" (NGR) stains use blended solvents and are sold only in liquid form. The virtues of NGR stains include transparency and fade-resistance, but their name is a somewhat misleading claim: Although these mixtures do not raise wood grain, neither do modern oil and alcohol stains.

Though technically not a stain, household ammonia can turn oak's amber color to driftwood gray by reacting with the wood's tannic acid.

Simply sponge copious amounts of ammonia onto the wood.

Testing Your Stain: Buy or mix the smallest practical amount and test it on a hidden area of the wood. Aim for a relatively light shade at first; it is preferable to darken stain by repeated applications.

If the wood in the test patch darkens excessively, you can switch to a lighter color; you can seal the wood before staining, to limit the stain's penetration; or you can use stain sealer, which combines a sealer with an oil stain.

⚠️ **CAUTION** *Rags soaked with oil may ignite spontaneously. After use, enclose oily rags in an airtight, flameproof can and throw them away.*

TOOLS

Plastic or glass mixing jars
Measuring spoons
Mixing sticks
Paintbrush (2")
Cheesecloth

MATERIALS

Stain powder
Denatured alcohol
Penetrating-oil stain
Turpentine
Nonpenetrating-oil stain

SAFETY TIPS

Wear rubber or vinyl gloves while mixing and applying stains. Work in a well-ventilated area when using alcohol- or oil-based stains.

Stain Types

Type	Recommended Use	Drying Time	Advantages and Disadvantages
Denatured alcohol	For wood with beautiful grain	15 minutes	Allows grain to show; fast drying. Fades in sunlight after many years; overlaps show up as dark streaks; not widely available.
Non-grain-raising (NGR)	For wood with beautiful grain	1 hour	Gives most transparent effect; does not fade. Tends to show overlaps; not widely available.
Oil (Penetrating)	For all wood	12-24 hours	Seals and stains in one step; flows and blends. Overemphasizes grain in some cases, producing zebra stripes or a candied look.
Oil (Nonpenetrating)	For wood with little or unattractive grain	12-24 hours	Obscures unattractive grain; produces uniform color. Gives opaque appearance; colors are not brilliant; does not cover well on hardwoods.

ALCOHOL STAIN

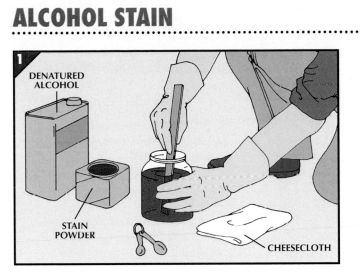

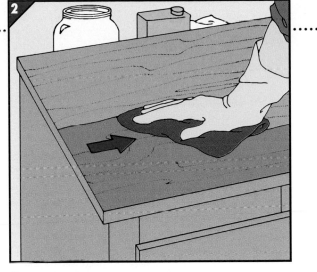

1. Mixing and testing the stain.
◆ Pour a quart of denatured alcohol into a plastic or glass container (alcohol might affect metal). Add 2 to 3 tablespoons of stain powder and stir until it dissolves.
◆ Dip a folded cheesecloth pad into the stain until it is damp but not dripping. Wipe stain onto a hidden surface and allow it to dry for 15 minutes.
◆ Examine the color and apply another coat or adjust the mixture as necessary, adding powder to darken it or alcohol to lighten it.
◆ Strain the mixture with cheesecloth to remove any undissolved powder.

2. Applying the stain.
To ensure that color is uniform, stain each surface in a single session.
◆ Use the cheesecloth pad to wipe stain on the surface in the direction of the grain. To avoid dark streaks at overlaps, wipe along the still wet edge of the last stroke, then quickly wipe away excess stain with another pad. Lighten any dark spots by rubbing denatured alcohol into the wood.
◆ Let the stain dry for at least 15 minutes. Build up the color by repeated applications.
◆ Allow the final application to dry for an hour before applying a finish.

OIL STAINS

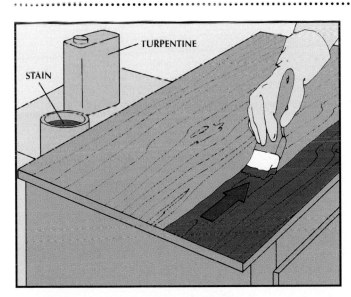

Brushing on penetrating-oil stain.
◆ Brush undiluted stain along the grain in even strokes. To darken the color, apply more stain. At overlaps, wipe off excess stain with cheesecloth wetted with turpentine.
◆ Allow the first coat to dry for 12 hours before applying a second coat for further darkening, if desired. Let the final coat dry for 24 hours before applying a finish.

Wiping on nonpenetrating-oil stain.
◆ With cheesecloth, wipe on a thin coat of stain.
◆ When the stain dulls, but before it dries, wipe away the excess with a new cloth. Let the stain dry for 12 to 24 hours, or until it is dry to the touch.
◆ Excess stain that dries on the surface may leave an unsightly opaque coating; remove it with a cloth wetted with turpentine or mineral spirits.
◆ If the color is not dark enough, repeat the application and let it dry before applying a finish.

Penetrating Oils

Easy to apply and maintain, an oil finish enhances the grain pattern and color of wood while protecting against moisture, dirt, and stains. The finish is simply brushed or wiped on, then buffed after it dries. It won't chip or peel, and although not as durable as varnish, it can be maintained with a fresh coat every year or so. Between these renewals, repair minor stains or scratches by rubbing them out with fine steel wool *(page 108)* and adding a little oil.

Types of Oil: Penetrating-oil finishes are available in two types, distinguished by resin content. Finishes with little resin leave almost no surface film when they dry; those with a relatively high resin content yield a hard, thin surface coat.

Low-resin products such as teak oil and Danish oil create a subtle, satin finish, intensifying the color of the wood and preserving the texture of the surface grain. High-resin penetrating oils may contain combinations of heat-treated tung oil, boiled linseed oil, varnish, or synthetic resins. When these oils are applied repeatedly, they build up into a durable, lustrous coating similar to shellac or varnish but not quite as shiny or hard. Because high-resin oils solidify within the wood, they increase its resistance to dents and scratches.

Matching Oil and Wood: Oil finishes darken wood slightly and tend to blotch softwoods such as pine, poplar, and gum. Before settling on a particular finish, buy a small amount and test it on a hidden surface of the featured wood. Be aware that linseed oil darkens further with age; it should be avoided if stable color is important.

Because the formulations of different penetrating oils may vary slightly, follow the specific instructions for the product that you select. You will need only a few tools: a 2-inch natural-bristle paintbrush, lint-free cloth or cheesecloth, and two grades of steel wool—3/0 (extra fine) and 4/0 (super fine).

⚠️ **CAUTION** *Rags soaked with oil may ignite spontaneously. After use, enclose oily rags in an airtight, flameproof can and throw them away.*

1. Applying oil.
◆ Wipe the wood with a soft, lint-free cloth to ensure that it is completely free of dust.
◆ Using a brush or lint-free cloth, spread oil liberally over one surface at a time. Wait 15 minutes, then apply more oil to areas on which the first coat has been completely absorbed and the surface is dry.
◆ Wait another 15 minutes, then wipe off all the oil with a clean, soft cloth.
◆ Let the oil dry for 24 hours, or longer if high humidity or low temperature slows the drying process.

A Handy Brush Holder

Instead of cleaning the brush and letting it dry between coats, make a temporary storage canister that suspends it in solvent without damaging the bristles. As a brush holder, you can use a lid from a dispenser for disposable cleansing cloths, sometimes called baby wipes. For a container, use a glass jar or a can. (Plastic might be melted by the solvent.) Poke the brush handle through the lid far enough so that the bristles will be immersed in solvent but not jammed against the bottom when the lid is set on the container.

If a baby-wipes lid is unavailable, use a coffee can and its plastic lid, cutting a $1\frac{1}{2}$-inch cross in the lid with a utility knife to hold the brush handle.

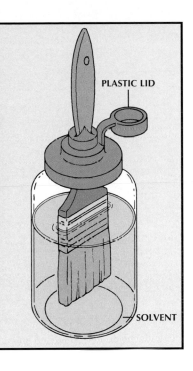

PLASTIC LID

SOLVENT

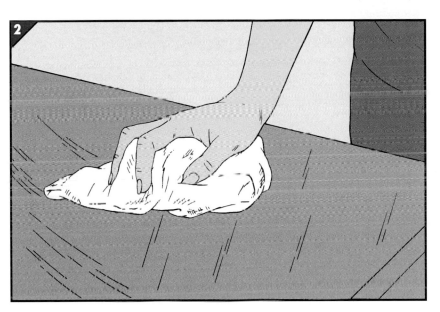

2. Polishing the finish.

◆ Rub the surface with 3/0 steel wool, working with the wood grain. Wipe off the surface with a cloth.

◆ Apply another coat of oil, allow it to dry for 24 hours, and rub it with steel wool. Repeat if necessary to build up the desired sheen.

◆ When the final coat is dry, use a clean, soft cloth to buff vigorously (left). The heat generated by the rubbing slightly softens resins and oils so that the finish can be further smoothed.

3. Adding luster.

Lemon oil will impart an extra-smooth finish to the oiled surface.

◆ Lubricate a pad of 4/0 steel wool with a small amount of lemon oil. Using light strokes, rub the oiled steel wool along the grain.

◆ Wipe the oil off the surface and allow the surface to dry. Polish by buffing in a circular motion with a clean cloth (right).

A Hard-Wearing Finish

Durability is often a key consideration in the choice of a finish for a bookshelf or cabinet. If you opt to paint the piece, maximum toughness is provided by two coats of primer plus a coat of a solvent-based enamel. Among clear finishes, the sturdiest is polyurethane. Because it is formulated with synthetic resin, polyurethane also dries faster than other clear finishes.

Polyurethane Options: Polyurethane finishes may be either solvent based or water based. In the past, solvent-based varieties could claim an edge in durability, but water-based formulas—with a far lower rating of volatile organic compounds—are catching up.

The procedure for applying solvent-based polyurethane is explained on these pages. Techniques for a water-based formula differ only slightly: Before you apply the finish, wipe the wood surface with a damp cloth rather than a tack cloth; and when you clean the synthetic-bristle brush, use water, not mineral spirits.

An Unmarred Surface: A clean workplace is essential when you are applying polyurethane; dust or other particles will spoil the finish. Work with only as much of the finish as you will need for that session; the longer your supply is exposed to the environment, the greater its chances of picking up dust. As a container, use a can or jar big enough to let you slap excess off the brush. Never scrape the brush on the lip of the container; this could create air bubbles in the polyurethane and also has the potential to transfer contaminants to the brush. To further guard against bubbles, do not agitate the container; instead, stir the contents slowly with a clean stick.

Best results are achieved by application of the polyurethane finish in long, even strokes. Three thin coats will afford maximum durability. Between coats, keep the container sealed.

⚠ **CAUTION** *Enamels and polyurethane finishes—especially oil-based types—are toxic and flammable. Apply them in a well-ventilated area.*

TOOLS

Dust brush (soft)
Hand-held vacuum
Tack cloth
Natural-bristle brush (2")
Synthetic-bristle brush (2")

MATERIALS

Polyurethane finish or primer and enamel paint
Dropcloth or cardboard
Sandpaper (220-grit)

SAFETY TIPS

A respirator and gloves protect against hazardous solvents contained in finishes.

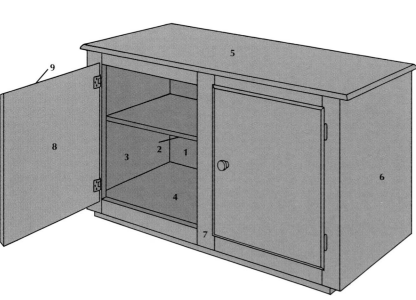

A cabinet-finishing sequence.

When applying polyurethane to a cabinet, begin with the interior and deal with one space at a time. First cover the back of the space (1), then its top (2), then the sides (3), and finally the bottom (4). For the cabinet exterior, the recommended order is: back, top (5), sides (6), bottom, and front frame (7). In the example at left, the back and bottom are left unfinished because they will be unexposed. If a protective coat for the unfinished portion is desired, use a clear resin wood sealer.

Doors, removed from the cabinet, should be done last. With the door positioned on level supports, cover the back and sides first (8), allow them to dry, then reverse the door and finish the front (9). Repeat the sequence with each successive coat.

A SOLVENT-BASED POLYURETHANE FINISH

1. Preparing the surfaces.

◆ Remove all hardware, doors, and any removable shelves. Place the cabinet on a dropcloth or on cardboard to protect the floor from drips.

◆ If the piece has been stained, make sure it is completely dry.

◆ Lightly sand the surfaces with 220-grit sandpaper.

◆ Dust the wood with a soft brush.

◆ Vacuum the work area, ending with the unit itself.

◆ Clean the surface with a tack cloth, wiping in the direction of the grain *(right)*.

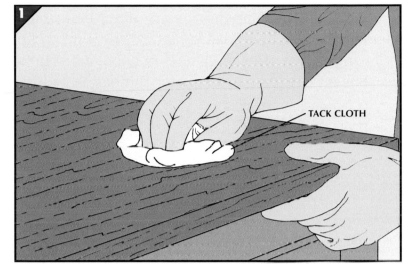

TACK CLOTH

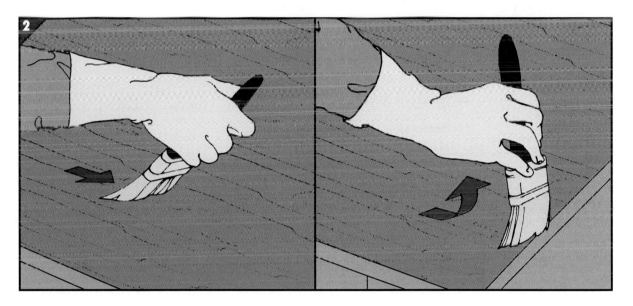

2. Applying the finish.

◆ Coat no more than half of a full-tapered, natural-bristle brush with polyurethane finish that has been stirred gently. Slap the excess against the inside of the wide-mouthed container.

◆ On horizontal applications, apply long, even strokes from the middle of the surface to each end, brushing in the direction of the grain *(above, left)*. As the brush reaches the edge of the wood at the end of each stroke, lift the bristles to avoid creating a ridge *(above, right)*.

◆ On vertical applications, stroke from the bottom up, to prevent drips and buildup.

◆ Remove any stray bristle or particle found on the piece

before the finish hardens; if some remain, dry, sand, dust, wipe, and recoat the entire area.

◆ When the surface of the piece has been covered, dry it for the amount of time specified by the manufacturer.

◆ Before applying the next coat, sand the entire piece with 220-grit sandpaper; vacuum the work area and the unit itself; dust with the brush and wipe the wood with a tack cloth. Repeat the sanding, vacuuming, dusting, and wiping if you are applying a third coat.

◆ On the final coat, remove any brush strokes or other imperfections by dragging the brush with minimal pressure from one end of each surface to the other end before the finish sets.

Appendix

Shelf and cabinet dimensions are often determined by the space available, but many other aspects of these utilitarian structures depend on how you plan to use them. The charts on the following pages offer guidance on choosing fasteners for anchoring shelves to walls, characteristics and grading systems for lumber and plywood, and pros and cons of various finishes.

Wall Fasteners   **119**

Selecting the Correct Fastener

Types of Wood   **120**

Plywood
Lumber

Wood Grading   **122**

Softwood Lumber Grades
Plywood Surface Grades

Choosing the Right Finish **124**

WALL FASTENERS

This chart of wall fasteners is keyed to the type of wall and total weight each fastener will support. To use the chart, combine the approximate weights of the shelves, their supports, and the objects they will hold, then divide by the number of fasteners needed to anchor the supports.

The sturdiest foundation for hanging any heavy object is a solid wood stud in the wall. However, if the wall has no studs—or if they are not conveniently located—the proper heavy-duty fastener will do the job. An expansion shield in thick plaster, for instance, will support weights far above the 10- to 60-pound figure that is shown in the last column.

Selecting the Correct Fastener

Wall Type	1-10 pounds per fastener	10-60 pounds per fastener
Cinder and concrete block (solid portions)	No. 7 to No. 9 masonry nail $2\frac{1}{2}$" cut nail Lead anchor with No. 6 to No. 8 wood screw	Expansion shield with bolt of $\frac{1}{4}$" diameter or larger Lag anchor with $\frac{1}{4}$"-diameter lag screw up to 6" in length for very heavy loads
Cinder and concrete block (hollow sections)	Lead anchor with No. 6 to No. 8 wood screw Expansion shield with $\frac{1}{4}$"-diameter bolt Toggle with $\frac{1}{4}$"-diameter bolt, long enough to pass through object being hung plus wall thickness	Lead anchor with No. 8 or larger wood screw Expansion shield with bolt of $\frac{1}{4}$" diameter or larger Toggle with bolt of $\frac{1}{4}$" diameter or larger, long enough to pass through object being hung plus wall thickness
Brick	2" or larger cut nail Lead anchor with No. 6 to No. 8 wood screw Expansion shield with $\frac{1}{4}$"-diameter bolt	Expansion shield with $\frac{1}{4}$"-diameter bolt Lead anchor with No. 10 wood screw Lag anchor with $\frac{1}{4}$"-diameter lag screw 2" to 3" long for very heavy loads
Mortar joints between cinder or cement blocks or bricks	No. 7 to No. 9 masonry nail 2" cut nail $\frac{7}{8}$" plastic anchor with No. 6 to No. 8 self-tapping sheet-metal screw	Not recommended: mortar joints crumble easily
Thick plaster (2" to 3")	Expansion shield with $\frac{1}{4}$"-diameter bolt Lead anchor with No. 6 to No. 8 wood screw	Expansion shield with $\frac{1}{4}$"-diameter bolt Lead anchor with No. 8 or larger wood screw
Dry wall or plaster and lath	Hollow-wall anchor in a size to match wall thickness Toggle with bolt of $\frac{3}{16}$" to $\frac{1}{4}$" diameter long enough to pass through object being hung plus wall thickness	Hollow-wall anchor in a size to match wall thickness Toggle with $\frac{1}{4}$"-diameter bolt long enough to pass through object being hung plus wall thickness (dry wall and thin plaster may collapse under heavy weights)
Wood stud behind dry wall or plaster	$1\frac{1}{2}$" to $2\frac{1}{2}$" finishing nail 3" common nail No. 6 to No. 8 wood screw long enough to be driven at least 1" into wood stud	No. 8 wood screw long enough to be driven at least $\frac{1}{2}$" into wood stud $2\frac{1}{2}$" common nail Lag screw or hanger bolt of $\frac{1}{4}$" diameter long enough to be driven at least $1\frac{1}{2}$" into wood stud

TYPES OF WOOD

The projects in this book are constructed with lumber, plywood, and often a combination of both. Lumber is used for narrow shelving as well as for framing pieces and trim for both shelves and cabinets. Plywood is used for the large pieces of a shelf or cabinet. For example, $\frac{1}{4}$-inch-thick plywood is often used for the back of a cabinet, and $\frac{1}{2}$- or $\frac{3}{4}$-inch plywood is used for the sides, bottom, and top.

Lumber and plywood come in two varieties, softwood and hardwood. The terms refer not to the relative hardness of the wood, but to the kind of tree the wood came from. Needle-bearing evergreen trees such as pine, spruce, fir, and cedar are the source of softwoods. The hardwoods are the deciduous species, such as cherry, oak, maple, walnut, mahogany, and birch.

With both plywood and solid lumber, softwoods are most often used because they combine strength, light weight, relatively low cost, and wide availability. Hardwoods tend to be more expensive than softwoods, but where fine appearance and durability are a concern, they are preferred.

For shelf and cabinet parts made of lumber, buy boards that have been smoothed, or "dressed." Softwood is available dressed on all four sides (abbreviated S4S), hardwood on only two or three sides (S2S or S3S). Both kinds of lumber should be kiln dried (Kd). Although more expensive than air-dried (Ad) wood, kiln-dried wood is less prone to warping and shrinking.

Plywood finished with a veneer of hardwood is suitable only for indoor applications. Softwood plywood, however, comes in both interior and exterior grades. If building shelves or cabinets that will be exposed to the weather, always use an exterior grade, which is made with glues formulated to withstand moisture and wide fluctuations in temperature.

Whether buying lumber or plywood, inspect it for damage before accepting it. Check plywood for nicks, cracks, and gouges in the surface veneers and at the edges and corners. Examine solid lumber for similar damage; sight along the edges of each board to check for various kinds of warping.

Plywood

Plywood is made by gluing together, under high pressure, thin layers of wood veneer called plies. The result is a panel that is exceptionally strong and resistant to warping. The plies are assembled in odd numbers from three to nine, with the grain of each ply laid perpendicular to the grain in the layer below. Because plywood panels always have an odd number of layers, the grain on the front and back of a sheet always runs in the same direction. It is not unusual for surface plies to be made from more than one piece of veneer. The higher the plywood grade *(page 123)*, the better the grains of the pieces match and the less conspicuous the seam is between them.

Type of Plywood	Species	Dimensions
Softwood	Fir, pine, larch, cedar, spruce	Standard-size panel is 4' by 8'. Thickness ranges from $\frac{1}{4}$" to 1" in $\frac{1}{4}$" increments.
Hardwood	Face plies commonly cherry, oak, birch, mahogany. On veneer-core plywood, interior plies consist of inferior grades of hardwood or softwood. Lumber-core plywood uses thin strips of solid lumber to form solid edges to better hold nails and screws.	Standard-size panel is 4' by 8'. Standard thicknesses are $\frac{1}{8}$", $\frac{3}{16}$", $\frac{1}{4}$", $\frac{3}{8}$", $\frac{1}{2}$", $\frac{5}{8}$", $\frac{3}{4}$", and 1".

Softwood Lumber Dimensions

For most sizes of softwood lumber, the nominal dimensions of a board are not its actual measurements. By longstanding custom now codified by lumber associations, the dimensions cited for the thickness and width of softwood boards refer to the size of the rough-cut lumber before it is dried and trimmed. As a result, the actual dimensions of the board are smaller than the nominal ones, as shown in the chart at right. This rule does not apply to lumber smaller than a 1-by-2. Such cuts are considered molding; they have actual dimensions equal to the nominal ones.

Nominal lumber sizes	Actual sizes (in inches)
1 x 2	$\frac{3}{4} \times 1\frac{1}{2}$
1 x 3	$\frac{3}{4} \times 2\frac{1}{2}$
1 x 4	$\frac{3}{4} \times 3\frac{1}{2}$
1 x 6	$\frac{3}{4} \times 5\frac{1}{2}$
1 x 8	$\frac{3}{4} \times 7\frac{1}{4}$
1 x 10	$\frac{3}{4} \times 9\frac{1}{4}$
1 x 12	$\frac{3}{4} \times 11\frac{1}{4}$
2 x 2	$1\frac{1}{2} \times 1\frac{1}{2}$
2 x 3	$1\frac{1}{2} \times 2\frac{1}{2}$
2 x 4	$1\frac{1}{2} \times 3\frac{1}{2}$

Lumber

Boards are cut from a tree in one of two ways, plain-sawn *(below, left)* and quarter-sawn *(below, right)*. On plain-sawn boards, the tree's annual growth rings in the end grain run from parallel to 45 degrees in relation to the faces of the board. Plain-sawn boards are fairly inexpensive and widely available but also more prone to warping. Quarter-sawn boards have growth rings more or less perpendicular to the faces of the board. The grain pattern of quarter-sawn lumber makes the wood less likely to deform and presents a more uniform and symmetrical pattern on the board's faces. Quarter-sawn lumber is not as widely available as plain-sawn, and is generally more expensive.

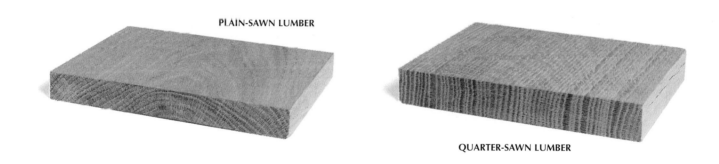

PLAIN-SAWN LUMBER

QUARTER-SAWN LUMBER

Type of Lumber	Species	Dimensions
Softwood	Fir, spruce, pine, cedar, larch	Nominal thickness of 1" or 2" *(chart, above)*. Widths nominally from 2" to 12" in 2" increments, lengths from 8' to 20' in 2' increments.
Hardwood	More than 20 common varieties, including ash, cherry, oak, maple, walnut, mahogany, teak, birch	Rough boards come in actual size of 1", expressed in industry terms as 4/4. The same boards surfaced on two sides (S2S) are $\frac{13}{16}$" thick. Other common S2S thicknesses are $\frac{3}{16}$", $\frac{5}{16}$", $\frac{7}{16}$", $\frac{9}{16}$", and $1\frac{1}{16}$". Hardwoods come in random lengths and widths.

WOOD GRADING

Softwood and hardwood lumber have separate grading systems based on the general appearance of the wood, including the number, soundness, and tightness of wood knots. A sound knot is an integral part of the board and is not likely to fall out. A tight knot has no cracks or fissures in it.

Hardwood arrives at lumberyards in varying degrees of finish, each with a different grading system; a knowledgeable lumberyard worker is likely to be the best source of information about such lumber.

Softwoods, however, fall into select and common grades, depending on which part of the tree the board is cut from. (Common grades are from the inner portion of the log, selects from the outer.) The grades are further divided into categories, as illustrated with ponderosa pine in the chart below. These grades are common to all softwoods except for Idaho white pine and southern yellow pine, which have different grading schemes.

Like lumber, plywood is graded by appearance, reflecting the number of defects in the surface plies. The grading is performed by industry associations that represent both softwood and hardwood plywood manufacturers. With softwoods, such as Douglas fir *(opposite, top),* the same grading system is applied to both sides of a sheet of plywood, so, for example, a sheet can be graded A/C, with "A" being the good face. Hardwood plywood (red oak is shown) uses a different grading system for front and back faces; the chart here shows the grades for the good face ply only.

Softwood Lumber Grades

Grade		Category	Description
Select		B & BTR (Better)	No knots or splits. Suitable for natural finish.
		C	A few tiny knots or blemishes. Suitable for natural finish.
		D	A few small, tight knots and blemishes on one face. More knots and blemishes allowed on opposite face. Suitable for natural finish or paint.
Common		No. 1	Larger tight knots. Takes paint well.
		No. 2	More numerous, larger knots than No. 1, some loose. Takes paint adequately.
		No. 3	Has splits and knotholes. Does not take paint well.
		No. 4	Large waste areas with numerous splits and knots. Almost unpaintable.

Plywood Surface Grades

Softwood Plywood	Grade	Description
	A	Smooth surface with neat repairs of blemishes.
	B	Solid surface with repair plugs, tight knots to 1", and minor splits permitted.
	C Plugged	Minor repairs allowed. Splits limited to $\frac{1}{8}$" width, knotholes no larger than $\frac{1}{4}$" x $\frac{1}{2}$".

Hardwood Plywood	Grade	Description
	AA	No knots or blemishes. Surface ply has well-matched grain and color between pieces. Suitable for natural finish.
	A	Smooth face with well-matched grain. Minor color contrast allowed. Suitable for natural finish.
	B	Smooth surface with some tight knots and minor blemishes. Less-exacting match between pieces.
	C	Minor streaks, spots, and variations in color. Minor blemishes and sound knots to $\frac{1}{2}$". No open splits or cracks.
	D	Unlimited streaks, spots, and variations in color. Repaired knots to $\frac{3}{4}$", 1" for sound knots. Minor blemishes, but no open splits or cracks. Amount of rough grain allowed varies by species.
	E	Unlimited streaks, spots, and variations in color. Unlimited small blemishes, but no open splits or cracks. Repaired knots to 1", sound knots to $1\frac{1}{2}$". Amount of rough grain allowed varies by species.

123

CHOOSING THE RIGHT FINISH

As endlessly varied as furniture finishes seem to be, most belong to one or another of the types shown in the chart at right. Always read the manufacturer's directions and suggestions on the product. Also consult the dealer. A reputable one should be well informed and able to advise you on your selection.

The various clear finishes such as shellac or varnish can be applied either directly to bare wood or over a stain. If you plan to stain, consider using a prestain wash coat to help the wood absorb the stain equally over the entire surface (below). After the stain has dried completely, seal it with a sanding sealer before applying the final finish. The sealer prevents the shellac or varnish from soaking into the wood, which would discolor the dried stain.

A prestain sealer.
Before being stained, the top piece of pine was treated with a shellac wash, which allowed the wood to absorb the stain more evenly. The lower sample was stained without a prestain wash coat, resulting in a blotchy look as the wood absorbed the liquid unevenly.

Finish	Variations
Penetrating oil	Oils may be blended, heat-treated, and/or combined with resins and varnishes.
Shellac	Used in its natural reddish brown state, the resin yields orange shellac; when bleached, it yields white shellac. The thickness of shellac solutions varies with the ratio of resin to alcohol.
Acrylic varnish	Available in flat, semigloss, and glossy lusters.
Alkyd varnish	Available in flat, semigloss, and glossy lusters. Exterior grades available for outdoor furniture.
Polyurethane	Available in flat, semigloss, and glossy lusters. Exterior grades available for outdoor furniture.
Acrylic enamel	Available in flat, semigloss, and glossy lusters in a wide array of colors.
Acrylic latex enamel	Available in flat, semigloss, and glossy lusters in a wide array of colors.
Alkyd enamel	Available in flat, semigloss, and glossy lusters in a wide array of colors. Exterior grades available for outdoor furniture.

Characteristics	Advantages	Disadvantages
Produces a luster and, with frequent applications, a thin film.	Easy to apply with good results; easily repaired.	Dries slowly. Not resistant to water or alcohol. Requires waxing for durability.
Produces a hard, transparent film. Orange shellac gives wood a distinctive amber hue; white shellac is practically colorless.	Applies smoothly when thin; dries quickly; sands easily. A good wood sealer.	Difficult to apply when thick. Many coats are necessary to give durability. Not resistant to water or alcohol. A top coat of wax is recommended to protect the surface. Loses its drying ability when stored a long time.
Produces a hard film that is notable for being crystal clear with no hint of amber.	Allows the true color of woods to show through and does not yellow with time or sun exposure. Dries quickly.	Because it dries quickly, acrylic varnish may be hard to apply unless sprayed on. Only moderately resistant to wear and spills.
Produces a hard, transparent film that darkens woods slightly.	Easy to apply with predictably good results. Suitable for all but the most heavily used surfaces.	Only moderately resistant to wear and spills.
Produces a hard, transparent film that darkens woods slightly	Excellent resistance to wear and spills. Easy to apply with good results.	Darkens with age. Hardness of the surface makes sanding difficult; to avoid sanding between coats, apply the subsequent coat within the drying time specified on the label. May not be suitable for use over shellac.
Produces a hard, opaque film that is notable, especially in light colors, for not having an amber hue.	Colors resist darkening with age. Provides the whitest whites and truest pale colors of all enamels. Does not yellow with time or sun exposure.	Dries quickly and may be tricky to apply unless sprayed on. Only moderately resistant to wear and spills.
Produces a firm, opaque film.	Easy to apply with good results; cleans up easily.	To avoid raising the wood's grain, apply only after sealing the wood with shellac or an enamel undercoat. Moderate resistance to wear and spills.
Produces a hard, opaque film.	Easy to apply with good results. Suitable for all but the most heavily used furniture.	Only moderately resistant to wear and spills.

INDEX

A

Abrasives: 108. *See also* Sanders
Adhesives. *See* Glues
Ammonia: as stain, 112
Anchors. *See* Fasteners

B

Backsaw: 9
Bevels, cutting: with router, 83; with table saw, 83
Biscuit joiner: 67
Biscuits: 66, 67; gluing, 67, 69
Block plane: 8
Bookcase for modular unit: 97; assembling, 98; materials and tools for, 97; mounting, 98
Braces, metal: 38; corner, 42
Brackets, shelf: building custom, 44; for standards, 41
Brushes: storing between finish coats, 115; for solvent- and water-based finishes, 116
Butt hinge: 84

C

Cabinets: anatomy, 58; planning, 58-59; scale drawings, 60-61; size of floor-to-ceiling, 58. *See also* Doors, cabinet; Molding
Cabinets, building: assembling box, 63-65; cutting components, 62; framing front, 66-71; materials and tools for, 62; planning cuts, 36. *See also* Drawers; Face frames; Wall systems, modular
Cabinets, refurbishing: 20; materials and tools, 20. *See also* Doors, repairing cabinet; Drawers, repairing; Shelves, cabinet
Carpenter's glue: 37
Carpenter's nippers: 24
Catches: magnetic, 86; single-roller, 86; spring-action, 86; touch, 86
Chalk line: staining by, 46
Cheek cut: 82
Chippers: 16
Chuck: drill, 14; keyless, 15
Circular saw: 10-11; anatomy, 10; use, 11

Clamps: C, 9; hand-screw, 9; pipe, 9
Clips: corner, 42; flush, 51; gusset, 51
Combination square: 8
Computer desk for modular unit: 91, 92; assembling and mounting, 95-96; desktop, 92-93; keyboard shelf, 92, 94; materials and tools for, 92; platform for monitor, 92, 94
Contact cement: 37
Coped joint: 107
Coping saw: 9
Curves: flexible, 8; French, 8

D

Dadoes: 16; cutting, 16-17, 81
Dado head: 16, 18
Dado joint, double: 73; cutting, 73-74
Detail sander: 109
Doors, cabinet: catches and latches, 86-87; frame-and-panel, 80; hinges, 78, 84-85; inset, 79; installing hinges, 87-89; lipped, 79; overlapping, 78; panel, 80; partially overlapping, 79; planning, 78; separated double, 79; stay supports, 85
Doors, frame-and-panel: 80; making frame, 81-82; making panel, 82-83; tools for, 78
Doors, repairing cabinet: adding latch, 28; deepening hinge mortise, 27; diagnosing problems, 25, 26; repositioning hinge, 28; shimming hinge, 26; unsticking, 20, 26, 29-30; warps, 26, 28
Dowel center: 71
Doweling jig: 71
Dowels: fluted, 66, 67
Drawers: anatomy, 72; building into cabinet, 65; construction front, 72; false front, 72; glides and runners, 72; replacing shelves with, 33; replacing with shelves, 31-32
Drawers, building false-front: 72; cutting double-dado joint, 73-74; installing glides, 75; making false front, 77; making guides and runners, 76; tools for, 72

Drawers, rebuilding: 25
Drawers, repairing: bottoms, 24; cleat replacement, 24; lubricating, 21; runner repair, 22; runner replacement, 22-23; unsticking, 20, 21; warps, 21
Drill, electric: 14-15
Drill bits: 14; brad-point, 66, 71; combination, 37; Forstner, 85; self-centering, 29
Drill guide: 48

E

Enamel, acrylic: 124-125; acrylic latex, 124-125; alkyd, 124-125
Epoxy: 37
Euro-style hinge: 85
Expansion shield. *See* Fasteners

F

Face frames: 66; assembling with biscuits, 68-69; assembling with dowels, 70-71; attaching, 70; basic rules, 66; biscuit joints, 66, 67; cutting, 67; dowel joints, 66, 67; materials and tools for, 66
Fasteners: nails vs. screws, 37; for various types of walls, 119
Featherboard: 13
Finishes: types and characteristics, 124-125
Finishing: dust removal, 108; and grain, 108, 110; with oil finish, 114-115; with polyurethane, 116-117; smoothing before, 108-109; using filler, 110-111; using stains, 110, 112-113. *See also* Molding
Flexible curve: 8
French curve: 8

G

Glides: installing for drawer, 75; installing for shelf, 99, 101
Glues: 37; applicator, 37; cleaning excess, 36; and fasteners, 36
Grades of wood: hardwood lumber, 122; hardwood plywood, 123; softwood lum-

ber, 122; softwood plywood, 123
Grain: 110; and cutting of tree, 121; raising, 108
Gullets: 11

H

Hand-screw clamp: 9
Hand tools: 8-9
Hanger bolt. *See* Fasteners
Hinges: butt, 84; Euro-style, 85; number and size, 78; offset, 84; piano, 85; pivot, 84; semiconcealed, 85; shutter, 84
Hinges, installing: deepening mortise, 27; filling screw holes, 28; on inset doors, 84, 88, 89; on overlapping doors, 84, 87, 88; on plywood doors, 84; repositioning, 28; shimming, 26
Hollow-wall anchors. *See* Fasteners

J

Jack plane: 8
Jig: board-edge centering, 49; doweling, 71; hole-spacing, 51; tenoning, 74
Joints: with biscuits, 66, 68-69; with dowels, 66, 70-71; fastening, 36; for molding, 107. *See also* Dadoes; Rabbets
Joints, cutting: 16; double-dado, 73-74; with router, 16-17; with table saw, 16, 18-19

K

Kerf: 11
Keyboard shelf: 92; installing, 94
Keyhole saw: 9

L

Lag screw. *See* Fasteners
Latches: bar, 87; finger, 28

M

Marking gauge: 94
Miter cut: 104, 105
Miter gauge: 12
Modular units. *See* Wall

systems, modular

Molding: 104; attaching, 104; bed, 104, 106-107; cut with router, 104; dimensions, 121; and kick space, 104; ogee, 104, 106; trim, 104, 105

Molding, installing: base, 105-106; cap, 106-107; coped joint, 107; materials and tools for, 104; scarf joint, 107

Mortise: making with table saw, 81

Mortise, hinge: deepening, 27; making for inset doors, 89; making for overlapping doors, 88-89

N

Nails: 37. *See also* Fasteners
Nippers, carpenter's: 24

O

Offset hinge: 84
Oil finishes: 124-125; applying, 114-115; lemon oil, 115; maintaining, 114; tools for, 114; types, 114. *See also* Stain, oil
Orbital sanders: 109

P

Piano hinge: 85
Pilot holes: necessity for, 37; drill bit for, 29
Pin, shelf: bracket, 51; spade, 51
Pipe clamp: 9
Pivot hinge: 84
Plane: block, 8; jack, 8; rabbet, 8, 30
Plate joiner: 67; use, 68
Plywood: 120; dimensions, 120; hardwood grades, 123; saw blade for, 11; softwood grades, 123; structure, 120; wood types, 120. *See also* Wood
Polyurethane finish: 116: applying, 116, 117; materials and tools for, 116; solvent- vs. water-based, 116
Polyvinyl glue: 37
Pores, wood: filling, 110

R

Rabbeting bit: 15
Rabbet plane: 8
Rabbets: 16; cutting with router, 16-17; cutting with table saw, 16, 18-19
Resorcinol: 37
Rip fence: 12
Router: 15; bits, 15, 83; cutting bevels with, 83; cutting dadoes and rabbets with, 16-17, 81; cutting molding with, 104; cutting mortise with, 81; variable-speed, 78, 83
Runners, drawer: making, 76; repairing, 21, 22-23

S

Saber saw: 10, 14
Safety: drilling into walls, 46; ear plugs, 16; with finishes, 112, 114, 116; gloves with chemicals, 110; goggles, 20; with power tools, 10, 16; sanding, 108
Sanders: block, 109; detail, 109; orbital, 109
Sanding: 108, 109; sealer, 124
Sandpapers: 108
Saw blades: circular, 11; for crosscutting, 11; dado, 16, 18; for plywood, 11; for ripping, 11; set, 11
Sawing technique: circular saws, 11; saber saw, 14; table saws, 12-13
Saws: backsaw, 9; blades for, 11; circular, 10-11; coping, 9; featherboard for, 13; keyhole, 9; saber, 10, 14; table, 10, 12-13
Scarf joint: 107
Screw holes: filling, 28
Screws: 37. *See also* Fasteners
Self-centering bit: 29
Semiconcealed hinge: 85
Set, saw-blade: 11
Shelf bracket systems: 41
Shellac: 124-125; as sealer, 110, 124
Shelves: planning cuts, 36
Shelves, built-in: 50; drilling holes for, 51; materials and tools for, 50; planning, 50; rectangular, 52-53; shelf supports, 50-51; triangular, cor-

ner, 53-55
Shelves, cabinet: planning, 36; reinforcing sagging, 30; repairing, 20; replacing drawers with, 31-32; replacing with drawers, 33
Shelves, floating: planning, 46; installing, 47-49; materials and tools for, 46
Shelves, freestanding: 38; building, 42
Shelves, wall: 38; installing floating, 46-49; installing single, customized, 43-45; installing single, on braces, 38-39; installing standards, 40; materials and tools for, 38, 43; planning, 38
Solid lumber: 120; board dimensions, 121; hardwood dimensions, 121; plain-sawn, 121; quarter-sawn, 121; softwood dimensions, 121; softwood grades, 122; warping, 121. *See also* Wood
Squares: combination, 8; try, 8
Squaring: cabinet, 64
Stain: applying with filler, 110; and finishes, 124; types, 112
Stain, alcohol: 112 applying, 113
Stain, non-grain-raising (NGR): 112
Stain, oil: applying, 113; non-penetrating, 112; penetrating, 112
Staining: materials and tools for, 112
Standards: and bracket systems, 41, 51; installing cabinet-mounted, 53; installing wall-mounted, 40
Stay support: 85
Steel wool: 108
Stud: locating center, 47-48

T

Table saw: 10, 12-13; blades, 11, 18; used for dadoes and rabbets, 16, 18-19, 81; used for mortises, 81
Tack cloth: 108, 109
Television cabinet for wall unit: assembling rotating/sliding shelf, 99-101; materials and tools for, 99
Tenons: cutting with router, 74,

82; cutting with table saw, 74, 82
Toggle bolts. *See* Fasteners
Tools, power: 10; circular saw, 10-11; drill, 14-15; plate joiner, 67; router, 15; saber saw, 14; safety, 10; sanders, 109; table saw, 12-13
Try square: 8
Turntable: 99

V

Varnish: acrylic, 124-125; alkyd, 124-125. *See also* Polyurethane finish

W

Wall systems, modular: 90; bookcase, 97-98; computer desk for, 92-96; joining modules, 101; molding for, 104; television cabinet for, 99-101; and wiring, 90
Walls: fasteners suited to types of, 119
Wash coat, shellac: 110
Wood: drying, 120; grading, 122; pores in, 110; types, 120. *See also* Plywood; Solid lumber
Wood filler for holes: 110
Wood filler for surface finishes: 110; applying, 110-111; materials and tools for, 110

Time-Life Books is a division of Time Life Inc.

PRESIDENT and CEO: John M. Fahey Jr.

TIME-LIFE BOOKS

MANAGING EDITOR: Roberta Conlan

Director of Design: Michael Hentges
Editorial Production Manager:
  Ellen Robling
Director of Operations: Eileen Bradley
Director of Photography and Research:
  John Conrad Weiser
Senior Editors: Russell B. Adams Jr.,
  Janet Cave, Lee Hassig, Robert
  Somerville, Henry Woodhead
Library: Louise D. Forstall

PRESIDENT: John D. Hall

*Vice President, Director of New Product
  Development:* Neil Kagan
*Associate Director, New Product
  Development:* Quentin S. McAndrew
Marketing Director: James Gillespie
Vice President, Book Production:
  Marjann Caldwell
Production Manager: Marlene Zack
Quality Assurance Manager: James King

HOME REPAIR AND IMPROVEMENT

SERIES EDITOR: Lee Hassig
Administrative Editor: Barbara Levitt

Editorial Staff for *Shelves and Cabinets*
Art Directors: Barbara M. Sheppard
  (principal), Mary Gasperetti
Picture Editor: Catherine Chase Tyson
Text Editor: Denise Dersin
Associate Editors/Research-Writing:
  Mark Galan, Tom Neven
Technical Art Assistant: Angela Johnson
Senior Copyeditor: Juli Duncan
Copyeditor: Judith Klein
Picture Coordinator: Paige Henke
Editorial Assistant: Amy S. Crutchfield

Special Contributors: John Drummond
  (illustration); William Graves, Craig
  Hower, Marvin Shultz, Eileen Wentland
  (digital illustration); George Constable,
  Peter Pocock, Glen Ruh (text); Mel
  Ingber (index).

Correspondents: Christine Hinze (London),
  Christina Lieberman (New York), Maria
  Vincenza Aloisi (Paris).

PICTURE CREDITS

Cover: Photograph, Renée Comet. Art,
Carol Hilliard/Totally Incorporated.

Illustrators: George Bell, Frederic F. Bigio
from B-C Graphics, Adolf Brotman,
Roger Essley, Jerry Gallagher, Dale
Gustafson, William J. Hennessy Jr.,
Walter Hilmers Jr., Fred Holz, Ron Jones,
Girard Mariscalchi, John Massey, Joan
McGurren, Robert Paquet, Jacques
Proulx, Dana Rasmussen, Kathy Rebeiz,
Michael Secrist, Ray Skibinski.

Photographers: **End papers**: Michael Latil.
**7, 8, 9, 13, 15, 29, 35, 37, 42, 49, 51,
57, 67, 71, 83, 85, 94**: Renée Comet.
103: Minwax. **109, 120, 121**: Renée
Comet. **122**: Western Wood Products
Association. **123**: Courtesy APA—The
Engineered Wood Association (3)—
Hardwood Plywood & Veneer Associa-
tion (6). **124**: Tom Wyatt for Sunset
Books, all rights reserved.

ACKNOWLEDGMENTS

Leslie Banduch, Porter-Cable Power Tools,
Jackson, Tenn.; Joni Bellerive, Stanley
Tools, New Britain, Conn.; Jim Daly, Daly's
Inc., Seattle; Teri Flotron, National Decorat-
ing Products Association, St. Louis; Larry
Goldsberry, Behr Process Corporation,
Santa Ana, Calif.; George Heidekat, Hard-
wood Manufacturers Association, Pitts-
burgh; Doug Jensen, Norton Abrasives,
Troy, N.Y.; Todd Langston, Porter-Cable
Power Tools, Jackson, Tenn.; Victor Lopez,
Behr Process Corporation, Santa Ana,
Calif.; Cathy Marx, Southern Forest Prod-
ucts Association, Kenner, La.; Franklin
Nichols, Nichols Woodworking, Washing-
ton, Conn.; Maryann Olson, American Ply-
wood Association, Tacoma; Sally Peck,
Hardwood Plywood & Veneer Association,
Reston, Va.; Becky Richards, Western
Woods Products Association, Portland,
Oreg.; Raymond Valentine, Smoot Lumber
Company, Alexandria, Va.

Second printing 1996. Printed in U.S.A.
Published simultaneously in Canada.
School and library distribution by Time-Life
Education, P.O. Box 85026, Richmond,
Virginia 23285-5026.

TIME-LIFE is a trademark of Time Warner
Inc. U.S.A.

**Library of Congress
Cataloging-in-Publication Data**
Shelves and cabinets / by the editors of
  Time-Life Books.
p. cm. — (Home repair and improve-
  ment)
Includes index.
ISBN 0-7835-3883-9
1. Cabinetwork. 2. Shelving (Furniture).
  3. Storage in the home.
I. Time-Life Books. II. Series.
TT197.S642   1995
694.1'6—dc20   95-983